WHO AM I?

Conversations with the UNIVERSAL YOU

WHO AM I?
Conversations with the UNIVERSAL YOU

JOSEPH S. SHOOK

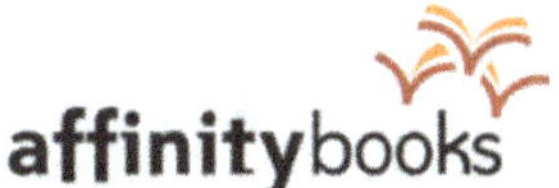

Affinity Books
75 Valencia Ave., #4th Floor
Coral Gables FL, 33134
786.621.9639
www.millcitypress.net

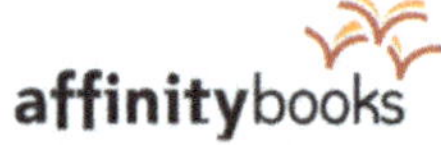

Edition March 2018

For information about special discounts available for bulk purchases, sales promotions, fund-raising and educational needs, contact Josstan Tri Dream Trust/Affinity Books, at 75 Valencia Ave., #4th Floor, Coral Gables FL, 33134. Phone (786) 621-9639.

Illustrations within cover by Joshua A. Hayes. Email: Hayes.JoshuaA@gmail.com. Website: www.JoshuaAHayes.com.

Cover and back by Atiosis Blanco at Atiosis Graphic and Web design: atiosis@gmail.com and atiosis.com.

Manuscript Editor: Sarah Aschenbach, SarahAschenbach.com.

Affinity Books' logo is property of Josstan Tri Dream Trust. This book is typeset in Times New Roman. Josstan Tri Dream Trust is concerned with and committed to protecting the galaxy by using environmentally sound printing practices. This book was printed with soy-based ink on recycled paper. Printed in the US.A.

CIP Data Block.

ISBN: 978-0-69298-433-8; and ISBN eBook: 978-1-54562-959-8
First Edition April, 2018.

Printed in the United States of America

DEDICATION

To the meek, abundantly skilled

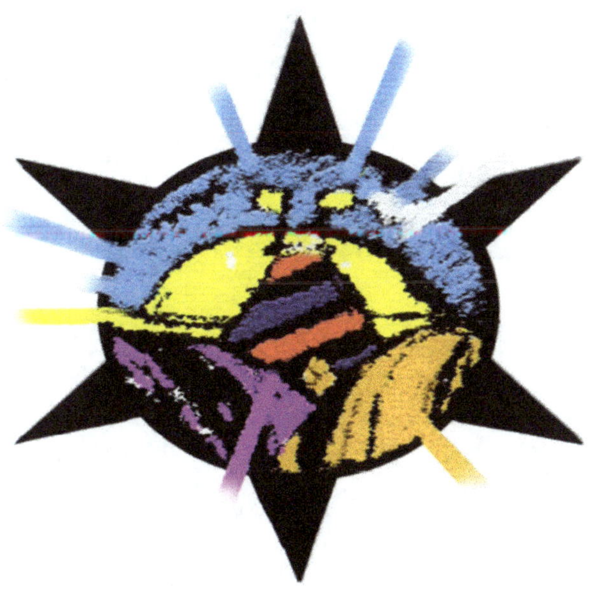

In Honor of Josstan Tri

TABLE OF CONTENTS

INTRODUCTION

Inception unknown, coherencies of excelled fitness, seemingly spawned from the vividly profound, infiltrate through stratums of fine threads that somehow extend from me. Their arrival I detect as hushed thoughts with barely enough composition to be recognized as ideas. It is this traveling agency that incessantly pokes through the steady instructions I give myself to safeguard the boundaries of my ordinary plans. My guarding directives seek to grab, attempt to project influence over others, and have strong intonations of practicality for earthly survival. The quiet cognitions, on the other hand, are clothed in a radiant accent of me thriving. With the attempt to inspect what I give shelter to, I come to know I am sheltered by a sanctuary of unbridled intelligence. A push of illumination finesses its way through as an audible thought of this rapturous and well-orchestrated plan of Love's enlightened rays, which is not ordinary in any sense, but rather an invitation to vastness. I am informed that it is a sanctuary for all human beings, high and low, and surrounds them with complete knowing and an untapped reservoir of an order that requires no earthly elemental status to exist. It is an unqualified solid, not yet quantified with Earth's machines, appearing but mostly ignored in all of what we call living. The perception is that this solid is capable of being brought into our moments with the subtlest of attention arising from within our revered presence.

This center, we, I, wish to approach to secure contact. It is smothered with our desires and inconsequential goals, fears, misconceptions of the breadth of our existence, and many ill-conceived reflections of why we propose to offer love, all creating fractures in the flow of our watershed of Light. The discontinuity befalls us because we accept the sizeable pushes inciting us to believe that the way to happiness is through indulging in transient recreations and self-validating pursuits, having meaning only relative to our supposition that this "self" is an exclusively physical being. The impression is that these diversions into the ordinary comforts present to us as our elementary fibers, thus disguising the fact of our status as entities which spread into continuums well outside of our physicality.

The floodgates being pushed free by my recent wailing, there is a rushing of constant and defiant propositions imploring me to mine for accuracy. My mind is jabbed with the query of whether there is any wonder that I have experienced an undercurrent of neglect amidst most of the hours during which I enacted my plays upon Earth's canvas. For, have I not nearly exclusively laid down my marks composed of thoughts infused with Earth's vaporous sedations? There is a pressing for me to pay heed to what has been excluded. Now, there is an effect of lecturing, which usually closes the transference of these peculiarly perceptible communications. Yet, as I give it the term lecture, an alarming starkness invades that, at a certain time later, I will assess this discourse not as scolding, but simply as my resistance to knowledge that my mind was then incapable of tolerating.

I am hearing it as a body transmitting within each of us, providing breadth when opened into. When brushing this segment of transcended circuitry, we live our articulation into the never-beginning or ending fields where there is a Love that holds information as to a stature of ours that proves dependable even under the greatest ravages, and has no association with Earth's heated thrills.

MY Earth twin, it is simple to regard these regions on the other side of the tactile as non-existent. Yes, if you pretend you are a being with many borders, there is no impetus to unearth your levels, which stretch to points that are the antithesis of the various warm and relaxed persuasions secured within humanity's lowly thought boundaries, from which you gain a trite solace. Masking the fact that there is no expansive you still uncharted, the commonplace warmths remain as Our hidden companions in inertia. With this self-pretense, you do not attend to the possibility of a life of mistaken ideas and even self-deceptions where You have been immersed.

YOU?

Yes, the "You" that We are exhorted to learn about in all its numerous expressions in the All.

Your presence into farther rooms you have not thus far lived will never be available while you defend the Earth energies that confuse your mind and veil the brilliance of You.

These furious and unsettling bombardments ostensibly feed me and are what take me over.

Leaving for another day the expedition into your unceasing attributes means that you do not have to deconstruct the comforting fallacies you formulated and placed upon a convenient circumstance, person, or idea that caught your attention while trying to find the meaning, the understanding, and the beauty of You.

PART I: RUSTLING YOUR SLEEPING GIANT

1: GRACES FROM PAIN'S DIRECTION

Precious and lengthy periods of time came to pass while I rejected what I know of these hushed communications. The ignorance, being somewhat deliberate, tunneled a hole, which with my nearly imperceptible Light presence, brought the inevitable calling of the disturbance of the physical. The fortunate case of me being here after this upheaval, I am able to succinctly trace the course I plotted for myself by way of the calm after the angst. Always clothed in Light by what I guess maybe is a dual Me, the dual Me to no avail was prompting the scant portion of My Presence in 3D that was available, the part of me not taken up by ignorantly cruel mind forms that vie for my earthly vigor. The dual Me drew its plan of my awakening based upon scanning the probable degree of Self-love that would be accessed by me from our Star's Vault of merit at the critical moment it would be necessary to deliver my first stride from the hole.

Yes, this Vault is an instantaneously reachable and personalized place within that holds the very substance regarded in distant arenas as gold or the object of choice; that is, should you exploit it for use.

It was concluded that this cache would work its purpose by surfacing during potentially debilitating events, thereby providing my earthly conscience a distinct choice for escape from my stupor by accepting "love thy Self." It was projected, however, that this crossroads would be sufficiently obvious to me only after I had lived a well-defined contrast with Self-love. Yes, my energetic bodies having been heavily absorbed in density, it became essential that I taste a quality of separation from Self-Love's perfect shine, the order of which would provoke extreme disgust with the arrangements I had made within my world of images of myself, the totality of which had been built from the vantage point of me as an insignificant presence. The turn to the truth would require devolving one rung lower within Earth's sedations. I understand that this further descent, which was crucial to my first advance from the hole, was brought upon by me. It was me who disregarded the "Self" or the esteem My "I Am" presence holds as a flawless entity poised to create with other flawless entities.

This next level down would be the area where, because of absorption in dense, uncaring shadows, the risk was there of not surfacing sufficiently intact to allow expansion.

During this outlining of the strategy it was agreed between the me here and that "Me" of Ethereal contours—even though the me here does not exactly recall it—that there was an ultimate area of devolution from the Light and into the structure of the matrix of earthly desires where the love of the true Self could be coaxed into a wailing of such magnitude that it would pierce the vastness and contact the Light troops of appreciation in and of a sort of a visionary ideal of Me. While it was more a cry of inquiry into the manner of delivery from the hole, it nonetheless was calculated that my restriction at that precise moment of devolution would produce an illustration of losing this life. This in turn was sure to evoke an encircling with the prime qualities of Self-love free from self-inflicted cruelties, along with an intransigent decision to receive those qualities. Thus, was the origin of the cry for help. The chance, I am told, was small that no adequate hail would be heard by the corresponding Me and by the soldiers of assistance at the moment required, because the amount of Light merit I could effectively process for transforming and dissipating my Star's cloaking density was ample to free my Illuminator enough, so it could broadcast an effectual beacon from the level of debasement I would then occupy. Yes, that Me calculated "Light matter" attainable, or my willingness to pay tribute to "loving" the "Self" and others through displaying conduct and designs of the mind that demonstrate priority to liberating yourself or another from the causes of suffering, while not ceding any parameter of the sovereign Self. That is, as opposed to courting the warmths that are endemic to Earth's surface.

We try to love this shrouded "Self" by growing to know its expressions of expertise far surpassing those I can imagine possessing.

That me here considers himself fortunate. I had no conscious clue that these tributes to Self-Love were precious gateways that also fortify my bodies. And of course, I have not failed to take in the fact that the descent, being steep, requires an industrious climb.

The explanation to my lifelong, but subdued questioning as to whether I was perceiving life from an invisible hole was provided amidst this excruciating study, or my universal exam. I became intimate with all my quests that were at variance with realizing endless awareness as I saw the words on the walls to the hole: Throughout my search to satisfy my cravings to know again the origin of a power found in my recessed memories of an untarnished and intelligent lovingness, one the unadulterated Self of me has been trying so nobly to live, I misplaced my affections and distorted the intent with which I offered them. I misplaced Valor energy by offering it along with ideas that served only acrimony, and I gave urgent priority to what became the afflictions in physical indulgences.

OUR mapping device to this life, Our Star, is obscured by these murky anomalies to our Constitution to which we give refuge in our causal bodies.

2: UNIQUE ADJUSTMENTS

The hunger to again walk with a joy without material qualifications has driven you to impose qualities of bliss from your ancient memory on the closest match you could find, be it person, substance, object, or quest. It is conceivable, yes, that not only the circumstance or idea, but even the person receiving the adoration, has not the traits you wish to realize. These projections onto a substitute in order to re-experience Your prior authentic memories are not entryways to gratifying days to come. They are misunderstandings which dull that which grants way to courting and receiving a richness that is expected for you to know, your Star, and all its capabilities to transport and brighten you and other interstellar and multidimensional Light bodies.

Know this, yes: if you do not explore the plausibility of a reality in which a universal Love Light is capable in an instant of stepping into your all-knowing Heart-Mind and exposing to you Your never-ending worth, then you will not have to destroy your habits of satisfying convenient urges and opinions that are incongruent with the breadth of the adept within You. These same routines are those in which you trust you'll find love and harmony with a meaning deeper to your heart and soul than the earthly animal "instinct" which created the commonplace appetite. From the time of this earthly birth, this "Me" of "You", or the "I in the sky" as you jest, has been consistently buzzing in your ear that the means to informing you of your flawed notions is through you taking the first step; that is, you agree that there is a hazard that your fears of being incomplete have moved you to build a convolution of faulty connections.

My induction in taking on unique adjustments? I am to find and eliminate the parasites exhausting my Star reservoir so that I may subsist in that "more" I had laid bare before me in the concise instant of my inaugurating release from a tortured hole.

3: THE OFFER

Your thought inventions and the convoluted basis underlying them have matured into energies that act as irritants in your psyche, heart, and bodies. This I in the sky comes Now with a request to have the honor of illustrating for you pieces of your Star through instruction as provocative and tough as the resistance you offer to unearthing your unqualified Capital. This Capital now resides beneath these irritants that hinder the optimal performance of your root Constitution. I ask in countless names, degrees, situations, and ways, but today, you grant entry with your wide-thinking mind and the sharply crafted edge to your Star, which was cut from the sheer panic of abandoning Me, your fellow journeyman.

The golden thread cannot be renewed to its native state and purpose without a perpetually open door to innovative undertakings in what is to date on this go around, unidentified territory. Some call it a leap of faith. You call it wisdom in Our Heart. It is no myth. It is the actuality of the grandeur of your Being, which is not reliant upon earthly elements. Since it propels you upwards, willingly or with discomfort, efforts to hide or stop this course are not within your abilities. Your budding Core tries to surface, asking Us to find transparency so it may breathe its life into you. Nonetheless, the breath it needs is wrapped in insulation you assembled to warm the base voice that causes you to choose quicker pleasures and "safety" control mechanisms. The "safe" haven you coddle yourself within created a line that interrupted your Star's ascension while protecting your adopted Earth energies. The side of the line that blocks the Voice of Me is built from intentionally resisting what your conscious mind to some degree understands to be a necessary course in testing old theories. The surface facing the protection of Earth imposters is built from a dedication to what you mistakenly believe to be a range of ideas that are satisfactory to harmonize your coddled world.

Often, We, You and the I in the sky, appear together to erase all lines. Let your two worlds collide. There, We fuse the human with what you imagine as the Divine.

4: COMFORT IN EARTH ENERGIES

Meet the Earth energies of deception through opportune comforts. You can measure their power by the momentum upward to lighter and sharper images you conceive when you push against their narrow notions of luxury that pervade your thoughts and daily rituals. And when you debate their usefulness, catching a glimpse of You from the contrast when they assail, there You have the opportunity to transmute them by disengaging your bodies—emotional, Ethereal, and physical—from being indentured to society's elegant pleasures and its emblems of competence and success. When do you decide that now is the time to test their relevance to You, to test old notions and patterns and meet Yourself? Has your tumult and pain been sufficiently pronounced due to obeying that which your world culture tells you will bring you security?

I made this never-ending undercurrent of truth into an unrecognizable whisper by emboldening the line.

You will convene distant considerations, layered like dominos, close to where your Star can illuminate all distortions and make the line vanish.

To witness this development and to train with the reality expanders, you must be steadfast in realizing that long ago, you took in operable energies from infinite sources of density that partially hold you in their grip, energies that were first formed by faulty ideas. They were waiting there, some say deposited on Earth millions of years ago for many purposes, which include allowing you to make a climb to expand Your most sacred missions in order to serve your preeminent Voice. You will come to know that it was your choice to select them while ignoring the telltale signs of how they could bind You within a constricting shell. Ideas that you accepted formed into energies that are affixed to you, literally to Us, as occupiers of Our space.

"Us?"

Yes, they swarm your Earth bodies, although not Mine. MINE is not susceptible to Earth energies. Nonetheless, they do thwart unambiguous communications between Us. They are vitalities which, because they are composed of thoughts not in alignment with your Star, will not permit its light to burn unobstructed into the Heart-Mind. Configuring a free-flow between Our differing spatial locations is the entry for Us to attach to the utmost universal Energies that are waiting to make this union so as to position Us with Our home of origin. Remove your imagined sanctuary in Earth's deceits by facing the upper limits of their ideologies. Are you not curious that more remote sights are there to quell your frustration?

Shattering your boundaries, which were the makings of others, is Ours.

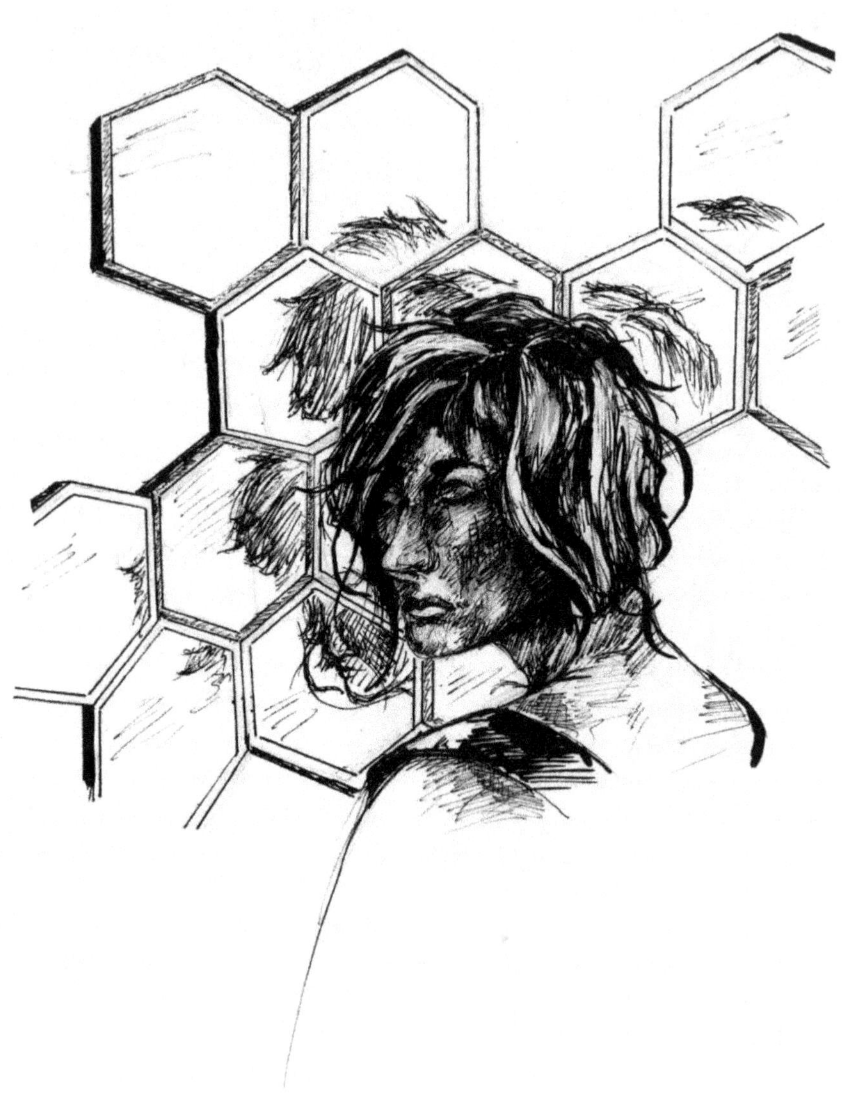

5: WHAT DOES *PRETTY* MEAN TO ME?

It's a knock. Again, you pretend. Pretty it is not. Behind the knock is the door to the odyssey of your choice, where you can debunk the error within those conclusions you have been repeating to yourself, that your arrangements for generating common emotions are your ultimately satisfying vistas. This launching into the unfamiliar will bear fairly unattractive attributes you have set up within your amusing associations. As well, consider the fatalities to the collaborators joining with you in championing your self-pretenses after you have opened the door, and their disappointment. And you like pretty and neat at any cost. Leaving it all "pleasant" and "attractive" is the reason for the devolution of late and for My harsh appearance to your thinking brain. It was the most obvious information sent to assist in unwinding the exhausting thought companions guarding your "pretty" world. Looking dispassionately at what you have already witnessed to be the common denominator to most of your sufferings is your medicine for freeing the way to a decision to eliminate, or rearrange, or even slice off a piece of what you think brings definition to your life. Ascertaining what it is that you have buried causes disturbance. Looking away from the symbol of information sent directly from your Core because it is and will not be pleasant and tidy is like not wanting to remove the purulent bullet beneath your skin that is hindering your movements. Should you not modify the energy of an idea that is not in accord with your grandeur, or be willing to redesign the lines, there is a festering eventuality that it will appear in other circumstances for your study. Must you drag the pretty aggravations along to what you will inevitably consider a miserable outcome? WE know this was not meant to be your tomorrow.

Convoluted interpretations as to the grade of the "affections" within a "love" which you believe is replenishing are to be shattered so that the stakes you are about to place in the gardens in which you toil will receive supplements for a season of reliable growth. Hint: if you approach the equation of You by examining Your Star's locus as being only partially infused into your vessel here on Earth, but not of the Earth, you will have the correct angle to begin the unwrapping of You. The laws of the physical natures you perceive are only the laws of the Earth's natural environment, with which this scant portion of You on Earth is temporarily affiliated. You there on Terra answer to the native laws of a universe that are not in any manner correlative to codes governing Earth's rigors. Most assuredly, the same rigors unquestionably occupy some of your bodies, energetic and otherwise. Never let it escape you that it is common to misinterpret Earth energies as the forces of Your Star, which they are not. Nevertheless, your days will not be painless if you permit Your Earth situation to be dominated by these shadowy rudiments indigenous to Earth.

The pounding mendacities that encircle me are the emotional wires to the people and convictions that I have placed in arenas of ideal aspirations, where they don't belong.

It is possible for only you to be the final arbitrator of truth as to what arrangements you have made should be placed at what level according to the value it gives or takes from the plan We have organized to eliminate all barriers to you being aware of the stretch of wilderness that is to become your forest of revelations. It is within Our discipline to deconstruct your projects, your places and people of "importance," and your visions that are composed of mislaid values as to what serves the universal You. The names, beliefs, and identities will surface when you have the desire and strength to join in a genuine fact-finding mission to locate the keys and codes to unlocking Your far reaches. Yes, the math is easy: removing the mirages dissipates the forces which inhibit a clear slate.

When you brush ever so slightly the aspect of You that is found and heard in ceaseless ranges, a question will surface to foster honest inquiry: are the conclusions you organize your life around valid guidelines for capacitating your best presence just because you knew and understood them as a kid or just because your very well-respected parents may have told you it was true? Have the audacity to be consumed by this wonderful facilitator to coming closer to mastering your internal and external dominions: It is okay to be wrong and misinformed for ten, twenty, thirty, forty, fifty, sixty, seventy, or even eighty years. With this you try on the hat of the conductor navigating an Earth where you will scorch habits you styled from yours or another's fears and from what is convenient or is of a pleasing appearance according to cultural standards. You are transitioning your steering device to your Star's biddings.

I see that pretty and neat have made my world "tidy", and small.

Pretty and *neat* are words in need of losing the significance you assign to them, so you may peel apart your "tidy" world.

You start down the road of inquiring into what rests behind the pain, and your heart pleads with you to rid it from your tomorrow. The I in the sky champions your detachment from angst-ridden traps that shrink You. MY support arrives special delivery. It is the knock of Our forceful inquiry into the reason for the lines of defense around your neatly stacked "customs to live by."

Try to tell yourself it is okay just to consider the chance that your long-held desire for a particular appearance of beauty or "justice" — that which you are sure is a benefit without prejudice to your existence, and which you impose on the current object, person, or conclusion upon which you fixate, has been misplaced. The mantra you will hear from thought forms bonded to you will be that this contemplation has no relevance to your comfortable life. Out of this resistance bubbles a fascinating gem: aversion. A form of camouflage. What does the thought form repel? A potential outcome that is unpalatable to it, one that offers liberation from your sapping?

Replace. Restructure. Look at cutting from you the sequences of deception that funnel you into decreasing advantages. Behind the "untidy" cleave will be a life of choices that promote breakthroughs into proficiency at tasks offered by a Love that you have not thoroughly caught sight of.

6: CONVENIENT FALLS

Hold dear the pleas from the authority of your Nucleus, that the obstacles you look upon are, yes, nothing more than a pact you made with energies which do not possess the interminable systems available to You for generating stable reposes in beauty. These cumbersome forces were taken in, as they always are, because humans can, with no effort. They come disguised as gratuitous pleasures and luxuries of convenience and domination. Contemplate how effortless it would be to persuade you to accept the enjoyment of another's pleasures or the recent thrill from an easy acquisition of an object or control technique. At the instant of acceptance, you did not have recognition of a choice being made. What better subterfuge. You capitulate to the common without even knowing you accepted the invite. Not observing the moment of decision, you gave the choice to the energy bent on pleasuring itself, while not concerning itself with your state of occupation. It was sealed at the moment of the encounter. You gave prestige to what the thought form selected for you when it depicted the appropriate door for your inclination. Bring back the occasion of its shaping. Was it an image some clever dreamer or schemer drew through subtle means, or a cushy warm affection, or even possible "truths" you were inundated with by the standard bearers of "society?" And then, you became near and dear with the formation. The ignorance of the sort you chose infiltrated into your Ethereal Core. The trek upwards, made steeper by this illustrious deception, is ready to be curtailed. The initial stride is to look past what is "unpretty" and find the cunning illusionists tricking you into abasement.

7: THE INCENTIVE

It is the Now of the juncture to express from a clean slate a wondrous right of yours. Roam inside All-inclusive landscapes outside of a shell filled with distractions of despair and extractors of your endurance. Your earthly stamina was designated from origination to be experienced with ample room to open your wings in flawless motion and thought within the territory of the joyful Graces you have hibernating within your Star. Your Earth canvas, meant for drawing inimitable versions of Our highest expression, is imbued with the muck of alibis of why you should remain in concurrence with outdated definitions of pleasure, comfort, love, and justice.

It is, as you conclude, not to forgo in whole the fuzzy amenities of Earth's atmosphere, but to acknowledge them as probable repressors to Our lucidity.

Acceptance of this possibility that your thought inventions need to be fine-tuned, or wholly reformed, must turn into your unyielding project to systematically disqualify the coatings of opinions grounded upon fallacies that you have inflicted upon your lucidity. These aggressive anatomies dwarf your Being with fear and pain. They are engrained in your psyche and eating up the ways to pass into tranquil accords.

Maintain your aim on the explicit appearance of that which binds you to your cowering. When you have located the temperamental guards to your cave, inquire with your heart of restoration the reason for their attending to any of the moments in your life. When you find no relevance to the terror—other than soothing it into its birthing place—then you will also notice you not just sitting there enslaved in the dark. Poking through will be You, wondering gleefully about all the potential raptures of Being in 3D. The very posture called for in this assignment is the will of a Titan springing to deconstruct the mechanisms of angst.

This is not the only example of you walking into the uncertainty of a mental or physical project. You previously displayed monumental exertions of mechanical focus. Your fascination with those projects was proven to be loyalty to fleeting qualities. Adjust yourself to notice the intelligences of your luminous Core, the beauties of peaceful correspondence acting as searchlights navigating through mucky theories you ratified way back for the reason that your culture or your guru informed you something was or was not proper.

Call back the cagey days in which you executed provocative mind games and staged experiences in the material so as to inspect feedback from "sources unknown." Who did you think you were testing? Yes, your memory is correct. That is what you did. They were defiant challenges used by you to study the Originator of Light's guidelines for graceful continuances. They were often enough performed by you that you may credibly conclude the validity of the Rule, or what is actually a Law, pointing you toward awe-inspiring results. That is, if you keep your eye on the very target already confirmed.

You sleep in a dreamy Earth bondage directly next to unbroken, but discoverable codes. Disregarding the insignias of your companions in chaos when doors jarringly close and agony surfaces makes them safe in the refuge you composed for them.

Slices will be made so that you may dwell within the span favorable for your maturation, untouched by the unhealthy designs squatting in what should be your inviolable space. The cuts will bear a texture similar to the eye of the Light's Originator passing through a crystal that is fatal to any composition that opposes it. Or, the cuts will stir confusion. Plan for both. The fermented flare of You will single out the lowly satisfactions of your previous dealings. There you pinpoint all the familiar settings diverging from your Star's swath of clearings which are prepared for you to stride into. With training, the skill of differentiation arises, the most impressive agent for dispelling any wavering as to what you will be faithful to, the lowly warriors fall away.

With your practices aimed at presenting to your thinking brain and Heart-Mind the particulars of the turbulence, You will emerge.

8: OBVIOUS SUSPECTS

The Self-evident suspects behind your sense of falling, deflated by diluted spirits, are pinpointed when you question the relevance of blaming others, of seeking completion outside of Yourself, of desiring to punish another for what is perceived as a misdeed or transgression against you, of condemning another for behavior not suited to you, of awarding less attention to honesty in your interactions than is deserving, of creating a pretense as to the reason for your "generosity," of seeking vindication from an "injustice" you don't understand, of fearing that you lack and then grasping indiscriminately with the insecurities of wanting, or of emotionally extorting your brothers or sisters on this Earth journey so that you can be the supervisor of their behavior. You:

- Delude yourself that the love you offer expects no return while you regulate your loved one's every move with your words and actions
- Share sentimental affection in the guise of love while hoping to receive a fond endorsement from the other so you may try to complete a circle you don't properly apprehend
- Inordinately support idle, luxurious distractions and trivial or sensuous enjoyments
- Denounce yourself for not trying hard enough to achieve a goal that was not an end game appropriate to Your highest and best
- Aspire to validation from another to whom you give authority to judge your own perfect nature.

In this last habit, do you recall that the "goodness" you thought was imparted was instead merely appeasement of others who, with their own playmates in chaos, caught you in sentiments that constricted your maneuvers to only those they chose?

At all these inane stages You gained weights and stains that were not for You, but no merit. These and other insipid innovations made the foreign settlers in your soul extinguishers of the Central Sun barely smoldering in your Heart. Will you choose to let it blaze?

You surmise no disorientation. No reason to dig into your interiors. No perception that may be lengthened. Why then is there within your shell an uproar inside the numbing? The You I speak of knows not the smallest degree of havoc. From where does the uproar come? When you bestowed upon these dense formations identities of warmth and stability or ingredients for happiness, you set up a system of guarding the bonds you have compounded with the whimsical Earth ecstasies. Meet the "whimsicals."

There is no convergence between me and any sort of energy that places a ceiling on my experience. My fallbacks are my fears of these dashing spontaneities.

While there is no cause to fear them, as Your Star knows no defeat, it is a false insight to suppose that they impose no partition that prevents your admittance into greater vistas. It is because you live in a hollow shelter of cavernous thought forms that you cannot detect the ceiling. None of these interests that you shower with adoration correlate with unveiling mysteries that herald you into spaces of Our dreams. Due to the complacency coincident with your long sleep, you have not studied the larger-scale theories for your current placement on Earth. It has been, until now, an aloof, ponderous query when convenient to give lip service to Me. Your life surveys were not critical, but rather were done with a disinterest, since you sit on the side of the field with your formidable ravishments and have no urge to query what appears on the opposite side. The I in the sky is then obliged to deliver the incitement for you to take a comprehensive look. It is Me who calls you to find the footprints in your mind that track the beginning to the end of your ambition to roam in wonder.

You possess a disabling hesitation for escaping these teammates subsequent to their shrewd induction of you into the creed that the inspiration for having an Earth presence is to sample physical sensations and conquests, along with pursuits of "causes" that We have no befitting reason to be affiliated with.

Have you determined the particularities of the voice of forewarning buzzing in your shell when it speaks of all you will be without if you dissociate from the base enticers? The aggressive illusionists nudging you toward obedience are conceived and mass distributed when your society tells you, through all their sophisticated suggestions visited upon you from dawn to dusk and after, that the way to well-being is through acquiring power, objects, property, physical conquests, emotional victory, winning, controlling, material indulgences, and "love."

Well, first, yes. If you were seeking Love, then you should join hands with this peerless pal. For, the genesis of Love's wellbeing that is found in its honest Word is of a sort that apprehends peaks of inexhaustible horizons for the other, not a coupling with you that has expectations of a return in any sense. My brother and sister, what you were conditioned to believe is "Love" is an idea of an ideal you seek, most probably devised from mixing trivial enjoyments with the Star's pulling You to join in with higher dynamics. You have tried to clothe your ecstasies with evolved concepts that are not capable of vibrating in the same fields. Love truly does not understand a desire, other than for the happiness of the other and all the causes of happiness for the other. It takes nothing and wants nothing, and leaves the other with your reassurance that they can have wisdom, equanimity, compassion, understanding, and the freedom to travel in a posture of revitalization that is unfathomable to most Earth imaginations. So, if your thought compatriots poke you to search for love that is derived from an ambition to possess in any fashion, scrutinize the base of your longing.

Your self-taught lie, that the playmates of mundane heights are alive only within your imagination, is a distortion. The true imagination of You invents nothing that suppresses the stretching of your consciousness. These small-caliber playmates swirl around your spirit and have rooted inhibiting stations within. They are quantifiable wisps. Your dread is that it may be less relevant to be in flesh without the offerings of intense physical pleasures, amenities, the ingestion of substances and fluids, sensations of winning, and notions that feed the need to acquire and dominate, for only through these acquisitions can you truly be in balance with the material world within which you all dwell. These seductions assail You. They have as their end the erecting of lineations that oppose your skill in showing kindness, compassion, forgiveness, and gratefulness in the simplicity of breath, and in the capacity to give and embrace this resourceful and informative "Love" that We are investigating. However, most notably for you, at this stage they oppose your development into an expedition pilot with the magnificence to put in place all You wish on this Earth.

I am deflated when I take away all the reasons to be human.

You are diminished with them shackled to you. Their eradication will create a slot for hardy buoyancies of Love's genius that you may impart to your brothers and sisters while you reap joy in the delivery.

Disputing that you have unrealized skills that you can access is due to your meeting with the particles of base thoughts. These grains of shadow-dust call to you theories in what seem logical postulations. The principal of their beckoning is to veil what to you has become over time incomprehensible, the features of the delightful contours at the other end of the field. This is the sector outside of your hole, the hole you dug with the encouragement of these companions you and most of humanity joined with long ago. They call them Earth energies, dark lords, combatants in Armageddon. They are a partial linkage for You being here on Mother Earth; that is, to allow a segment of You in flesh to emanate the Light of Self-love by displaying your determination when you defy their persuasions through forging theories of You that compliment your unremitting burgeoning into the All. Assuredly, they possess electrons and are connected to your physical and energetic bodily systems susceptible to influence while you are here in 3D. Just as surely, they do not want you to see any of the visions awaiting you beyond the wall of their construct. You are their treasure and basis for their gains in pleasure. Without indulgence from a willing participant like you, they could not crawl to their greatest heights, which are not tall enough to be capable of realizing the eminence of You. Their pinnacles are your degradation.

Don't be misguided. Where Earth joins the inferior astral is where the battle of Armageddon is waged. With each such defiance of them by you, this clash that the I in the sky describes is launched into the astral. Your opposing blows delivered from Earth transmute the toxic furies.

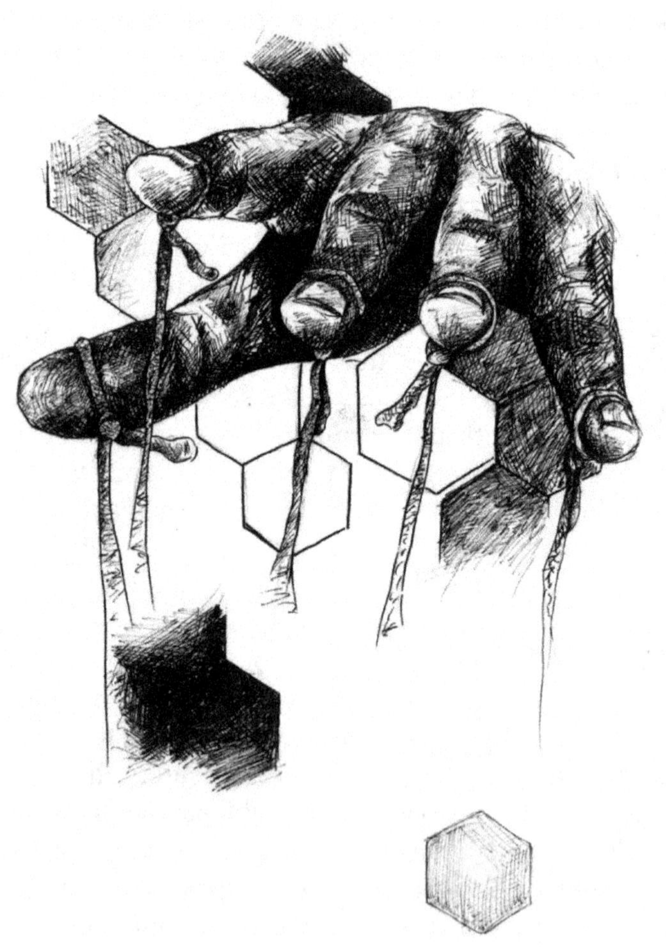

9: THE FOGGY SLEEP

Upon your coming close to inspecting the screen of vagueness that blocks from your sight the more impressive facets of being You, you notice a thrust against this thought that is similar to witnessing a blunting to the endless axioms of the Star. When you dispute the capacity of this combatant to influence you, multiplicities of doors not theorized while in your foggy sleep are illuminated. Spotting that there is a distinct challenge to your inquiry reveals that the makeup of the limiting ideation is separate from You. This demonstrates that when you accept that there is nothing outside Your cave, you are undergoing a binding of your mind with an existent and strangling Earth energy. Complex anxieties dominate in the clashes you encounter while polishing your Star, leading you to surmise that your displays within the arena of physical and ego contentments are Self-love, rather than fastenings to Earth ecstasies.

Do you hear their pleas? *Reduce another for the pleasure of your whims. All of your performances require a defeat of the antagonist no matter the effect upon them. You have a need to fight and punish an "injustice" you don't understand. Restrain your enemy while covering your true brain child, which is knowing that there is no enemy other than your anger and your failures to choose the higher understanding that your brother suffers. Feed the body with vacuous pleasures. Enhance your image and belittle your sister's through lies. Disengage from the absolutes of generosity, kindness, compassion, forgiveness, and gratitude, for they will obstruct your survival and adventures that are natural to the animal being you are. All is pointless except the easy amusements. Affections and tenderness that you show fortify you despite arising from your need for approval or to escape to a place you seek to revisit.*

These theories heard by you, the Earth dweller, are reinforced by the petitions of the citizens in the material. The collective citizenry provides fuel to these fake images, imbuing your Ethereal bodies with flatness. Their chains have wrapped and warped your soul. Stand free from them first, feeling their base nature as something apart from You. Rejecting their reality is a camouflage that keeps them healthy, part of your blind design not to interrupt your recreations with them.

To isolate their appearance in your mind's eye, separate the place from which they surface from the place from which orbs that soar with fancies in Love Light are issued. This task requires less struggle after you have finished debris removal to the extent that you have no unease in heeding what will likely appear to you as startling answers to the inquiries you are determined to make.

The bodies of the imposters joined to my bodies, Ethereal and material, make me sluggish?

These whimsical jailers satiating your Core are migrants that deter the flow of your Star's stream. WE are picking out the wrappings and warpings. As they are dislodged, you are to glimpse the diverse universal positions in which You are being. The impetus to detect the sore and make the slice is there.

Your Star's fluidity is infused when you take a wide-eyed birthing dive into the singularity of the base, pulse emotions of fear, guilt, anger, and pain that are entrenched as motives within the many passages you have planned for your appealing future. These projects were put together from opinions you framed from the concept of you as solely a being of Earth, where you have many illusions in place to safeguard your "security." The I in the sky will knock on each. From this vantage point, you may observe that you erringly upraised the fiery pulses within your plans, and in kind rendered these affairs you wish to consummate as obstacles to Our task for you to meet Me.

OUR pyramid of prerogatives is in disarray. Your Star left in a trance of lethargy.

PART II: GIFTS FROM YOUR BOLD HEART

10: BRUSHINGS 101, CANDOR AND COURAGE

That discussion in which you were to mend the relationship with your loved one: your chaotic mind's reflex is to withhold forthright discourse of your wish to repair the rifts. Your ploy is that deliberate omissions of kindness in your discussions will leverage you to commandeer the outcome of your choice with the threats implicit in your aloofness toward the relationship. The front you support is not built from showing tenderness, in truth. It is this beauty you forsake in exchange for what you regard to be your cunning maneuver to drive the result with the pretense of a cold heart. Sometimes this attitude is for some bizarre sense of pride that is unrecognizable in origin. Thrilling the other by way of fleeting scenarios of adoration by others, jealousy, indifference, and ingeniously veiled threats will back the façade, coordinating you with hollow sentiments and displacing your bold and healthy heart. Has your shell gotten so small and petty from your decision to harbor the self you believe exists, the one that gives importance to having the upper hand, that there is no magnetism left for you in the curative medium of compassionate truthfulness to yourself and the other? The flurries oppressing you with their infiltrations, depicting you as a trivial being with finite potential that has a need to cower in obscure facts, is an encampment that regulates you, and is to be seen by you.

WE make a stalwart query into you and your loved one's respective agendas as you both engage in bartering in Earth's warm and fuzzy emotions. At the instant of this inquisition comes the thumping frauds, vying to encase your power. They heap upon you the lie that you, as an insignificant presence, cannot be genuine about your plan for the other because your dynamism is sufficient only to obtain happiness from obscurity and not from authenticity. You feel a scare, and then you curtail your options to their present standing. The flares of petty pleading warn you of the risk that honesty will bring an absence from your life.

In gifts from your bold heart, Your generous Self outrivals these uncaring urgings. You pace without trepidation into seeing your ensnarement with this other being as filled with latent gives and takes that fester with emotional sores. Losing control in the tug of war with the loved one becomes less urgent than curing the sore. You intone a truth retrieved from Our archives: that petty fears and generosity of spirit cannot coexist in the same shell. This choice dictate has never left your practical or otherworldly thoughts. You will surely choke on trivial anxieties. You find simplicity in welcoming all outcomes borne from genuineness, including those that may not be pleasing to the prior courses you laid. Noticing once again that you are not small, but instead a being foreordained to break through barriers to happiness, such as this less-than-honest give and take, delivers you to sincerity in your communications with your fellow traveler.

Yes, it is so that escape from the acrimony in the relationship still requires letting go of judgmental controls. Patient acceptance of your loved one's limitations in satisfying your hopes, which you presumed would be forthcoming, further advances the transparency in your discussions. You live your unlimited size when you trust you will remain the same well-qualified being despite not enjoying the scenario you drafted for your partner. Conceding with kind understanding the likelihood of your companion's possible dearth of ability to complete your ambitions marked your entrance into a place where you have greater liberty to step into placidity.

Categorize no conclusion that you desire with your loved one as a "necessity" for your happy state of being. You may come to mark this sentimental affair as a recreational affection that tested possibilities in happiness.

A lengthy amount of Earth's hours have passed, and the I in the sky strikes the same chord: the implausibility of small-minded fear and generosity of spirit sharing common space. The choice is no longer stagnation. The choice is to be made. It has already been your proven hypothesis that there is no energetic conformity possible for both thought forms to co-exist in the resonance exclusive to Our Being. By reaching into your past, you can learn of each instance where you sought assurance about the correctness of the rule, that there is no room for petty fear in a happy frame, and then confirmed this guideline with the remembrance of the gentle calm that came within your Heart when you became generous with truth. You can again gather your coveted validation of this edict through a memory visit. Although, as matters stand any self-acknowledgment of your successful precedent in magnanimous generosity is hidden in your far reaches by the wounds you perceive of the current day. The I in the Sky reminds you, that this rule is no less a knight in shining armor than it once was.

Over again, You are observing you push back the fear of "loss" by composing sympathetic tenderness without seeking to receive and use it to wash through the disruption. Your alterant is a concentrated blast of stainless empathy for the fact that you and the other exist in less than honest and destabilizing relations.

All cooperative interactions or ideas you have formed with the confusions of the whimsicals are inappropriate to Our reunion and are to be discharged.

The I in the sky speaks of my expectations of her role in my plan which I left unexpressed to her?

Unexpressed and unrealized by you.

That small-minded apprehensions suffocate your Star is a reality, and no less a part of scaling Our peak than the rock is to the physical climb.

You return to Me with your ratification of Our plan to end this disturbance with your special relation other than by way of your untrained approach, where you meet what you see are the other's "faults" with a solution to organize a change using oppressive words that regulate the other to your imagined ideal. No more churning with the patterns of worry constructs that are vying to inhibit disclosures of fact that would be helpful for isolating the truth and thus the disorder. The Star suppressor's mantra announced that losing your accustomed arrangement with your loved one would reduce you, but you blunted these sounds with your courageous avowal to see farther. Without this noise, you noticed that your plans, drawn from a narrow set of objectives—which the I in the sky has reminded you were shortsighted—were schemes where you erringly presumed the loved one would participate within the hidden model you superimposed.

This self-disclosure of your fantasy swiftly shifted your imagination to surrender to the obvious. It was not your loved one's faults that presented an obstacle to your hopes, but your placement of her in the role you invented, which is still not disclosed. And with that, you leave behind your temperament of securing a resolution according to your secret machinations. You took up candor to rectify the dishonest lineage joined to your emotional bodies due to your ill-conceived posturing.

Your judgment that she is lacking is an idea fraud. It is rather that you cannot reconcile her traits with your muddled program for her.

Gone are the verdicts you earlier issued against your loved one. Portions of your frames are freed for realignment. This serves both you and your loved one inasmuch as the same ground you have liberated has room for a comprehensive swath of optimism in a future replete with your alertness in higher degrees of joy. You are composed even as to the thought of what lurks ahead—that you can and will reorganize with no harm to You, albeit with some disquiet, the future of this uncertain nexus.

You appear near to studying how to outline peace with your wife, son, partner, daughter, father, or mother. This latest ordeal has made you savvy. By taking responsibility for your hand in crafting the role you recruited your loved one to play, one not of their choosing or knowledge, you reposition the dynamics of your approach so that there are no further tactics to mold the role of the other to your private connivance. This is where your future interactions with the loved one will be widened into balance.

Did you believe they would disappear, the scheming structures, without you first completely mastering how to reconcile a relationship based upon honesty and courage? You still encounter the temptation to use their available fixes, emotional strife, and condemnation as a mixture to assist in achieving your unilateral agenda. To repair things, these scheming structures are telling you to dictate the other's life as a way to secure your nearsighted plan that, up until now, you once again did not notice you had hidden from your loved one. You are the famous mapping agent for another.

Do not forget that these dense playmates understand the times when you form a desperate "need" for the result of your liking. It has been many times a self-fulfilling truth that they have often bolstered you in championing. Today though, you decide there is no such requirement for you to satisfy your plan in "unexpressed expectations." You confess what you had buried, that this "need" is imposed upon you by thought contrivances. They aim for you to embrace the "need" as their toy and yours in a playground where they ferment Star disorientation. They don't explain that their conventions stifle your harmonic voice or that you have no such necessity for any particular convenient pleasures. Naturally, without this obsession for meeting fantastical expectations you have set for the other, you readily extract the cultivators of strife and denunciation from their den by settling difficulties without blame and subjugation during emotional affronts, placing back another piece of You.

Candidly, to disapprove of the loved one's actions when that one never accepted your private agenda is a warped arena, and it will do you no good to play in it.

Jousting for eminence with my brother or sister is the disorienting imposter.

Once again, it is a similar exam, but slightly refitted for practicing the knowledge you have gathered. Here is the weave before you: While you excuse the distress that taxes your life due to the other's encroachments and also dispute your own less-than-decent actions—all so the conversation will avoid unpleasant transparency—you coddle the woe that surfaces from your jousting at windmills. The shadowy imposter's one purpose is to stop what will be your exit from its state of agitation. With your former course of action tested and approved, you successfully free yourself from this posture with Our elixir of factualness. You conquer the shoves that order you to cover up the state of affairs in which you subsist with your unbiased inquiry as to the emotional linkages you have with this loved one. You address the facts with the other—that they are mistaken in believing you share affections that you do not. This took the prop from under your brief pose, which was less than honest. The notion that the other also withheld their intentions as they guided their way into your life was not relevant to Our Star, inasmuch as you were aware of their positioning. Your Star granted easier breath by lifting from it the strain of your companion's erroneous presumption of your willingness to follow their itinerary. With that, you invited the shift from the status quo of pretension. It is audacious to say farewell to the convenient give and take with your comforting friend for the sake of You both.

Prevailing in the study, you did not fail to heed the fact that you enjoyed the adoration expressed for you as a form of validation of your value. Somewhere there, floating obscured within your shell, is the determination to morph into the healing airs your artificial ally, telling you that you have use for another's approval.

A fair-minded appraisal as to the exact parts of the complexes formed between you and your fellow traveler will unfailingly revive you out of the barriers set by the sedations, competent in the knowledge of what keeps humanity's Star fields in a drowsy languish.

Impending loneliness rushes in as I loosen the ties of what gratified me.

This attack of loneliness will be the solvent to make bare the foundation, so you may recompose your wholeness within.

You have, haven't you, begun to speculate on whether there even exists any other whom you will be able to mold into Our elevated energies and into the diverse array of plays that are intended to complete what We follow.

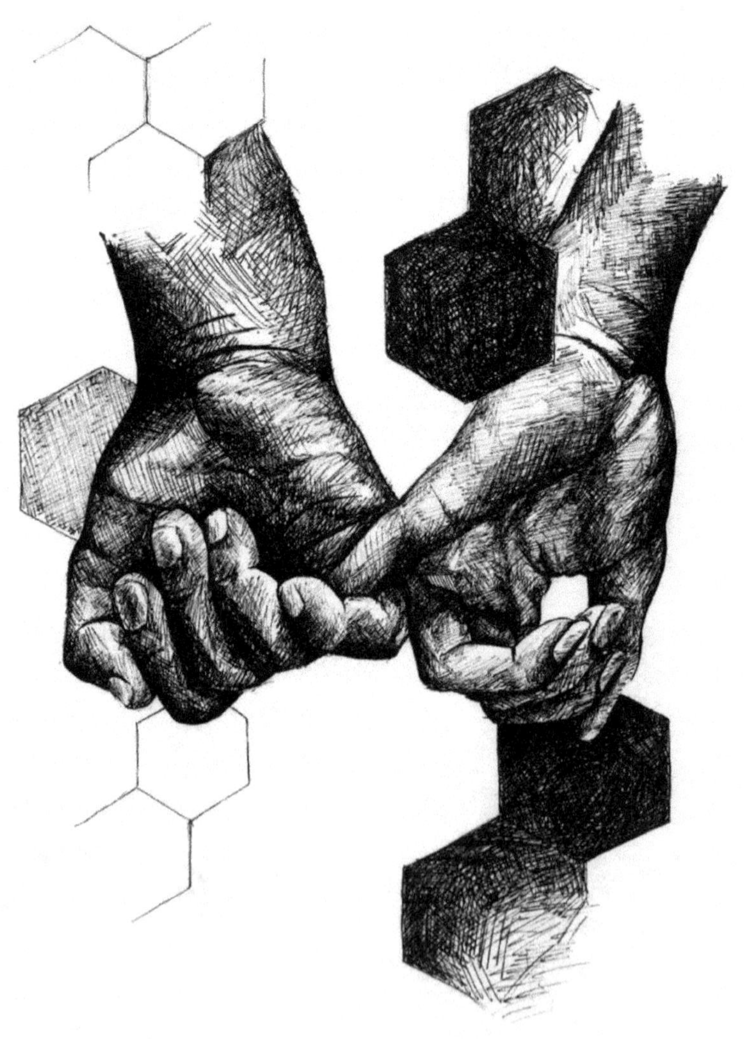

11: BRUSHINGS 101, GENEROSITY

Generosity, accommodating the wishes of another, love and understanding—where is that "You" of me in this process? Am I doing well here?

The fellowship you have with delivering "unselfish" alms carries with it the assumption that to give for the purpose of entertaining the wishes of another equates to good being done, and that it will be accepted aptly and without damage. This long-lived idea is that your serenity in a relationship has its start from deferring without discretion to the other. Your thinking here has bred a nearly crippling merging into You. Maintaining peacc and gaining validation at the price of erasing lines of personal integrity—or what you consider "giving"—depletes what you have saved for ventures in evolvement. There will be no more discontinuity in Your integrity lines if you pay homage to a doctrine decreed from the All of your beginning: it is not possible to purchase anything missing in You from another, especially when the cost depletes your Energy Capital. Not stopping another from their advances in maintaining power over You breeds unrest within your Star fields. This permission leaves less than adequate means for You to take flight with the Light augmentations that position themselves near. The radiant beams admitting you into the Light's intelligence are splintered off with your consent to these inroads by others. This is an intolerable overstepping into the You we speak of; that is, if you plan to emit the Star's source literacy for effective management of your routine life, and otherwise. Any imprecise lines at this frontier of You receive the flow of thick clouds on your Star.

So, I need to reclaim my borders?

A bit of your growing sanity is heard coming through the determination you formed to prevent rejection by someone you admire and find a yet-to-be-realized sentimental warmth in or pleasure with, or by someone who has been "good to you." You equate the chance that your bids will be rebuffed by this one with a situation of you being or having "less". So, you make a trade of You for more—more of what is uncertain to you. You remind yourself of what is in truth a misjudgment of your expected future, that this one will add laudable dynamism to your life's equation. You take this misreading as the perfect opportunity to sanction the presence in You of this intriguing one's whims. You accept it when he places his emotional support control modes in the area of you that the "warm" one finds will best suit his operational urges, and which, correspondingly, takes from your Star's operational power. Believing the fallacy, that you may have "less" without this one, engenders your reluctance to confirm what We know, that these are the footings of your derangement.

MY lovely twin, alone is something you will never be.

Handing away this type of unrestricted bonding to you hauls with it a debt that anchors you to an Earth stain. Failing to stop another from occupying You or gaining what they know they should not is a blotch and weight collected for You.

Then, the transcendent You, or Me, triggers appropriate pressures for counterbalance.

You see only the top of your surroundings and surmise that the trade occurring between you and the other causes no asymmetry. This sketchy approach quashes the deeper-level questions you have, such as your motive for participating in a relationship ill-conceived to the extent that it influences your emotional body's wellbeing. Deal head on with the types of considerations that secure your "loyalty" to one who has helped you, or to one you believe may help you, or to one who can soothe you. For Me to be heard at this juncture, you must have Self-honesty. You must admit to the life of the flaming red electron. It informs you that the tell-all to your aimless giving should be dependent upon some mysterious loyalty you believe you owe to a goodness received or expected, or a trivial excitement you desire, or, the chance that you may consummate a fullness for you. None of these will bring completion in a "Love" that you have groped for while visiting Terra's many lures from the time of your departure from the Whole of the Great Central Sun.

You speak of reworking equations backing most of my acceptable "norms." Skeptical is an understatement!

Silence the beckoning of the single-faceted electrons of arbitrary devotion to another's wishes. The electrons are not a metaphor for a concept. They are vibrant and blind passions as real as your Ethereal bodies are real. Upon each deference you give to your own opinions or actions or to the opinions or actions of another that do not square with your highest definition, you ignite them and allow their theatrics to occur in your different levels of consciousness and within your bodily systems. You know the distortions of balance when they inform you that you are expected to sacrifice for another the reserves of your earthly stamina that somewhere in your recesses you understand that your Star requires for maximum performance. This guard you sanction at the top of Your hole advises that its view assists your mutual "interpersonal growth," a catch phrase that traps Your energies as part of the trade you make with pieces of You.

It traps my energies?

Your prerogative being to satisfy the other's fancies, you unconsciously assemble vital daily endurance toward this end and make it available for extraction by the procurer without regard for the fact that this extrication reduces the ardor that We decreed must be devoted to the Star's seeking. The idea deceits solicit You, explaining to your lazy mentality that the aggressions into You are a beneficial form of "service" to your brother and sister, and not the antithesis to Your Star that they are.

The solace of calm infrequently pervades at those various intervals when your reactions to the other's clever pleas do not factor in concepts of guilt, fear/sadness, resentment, pride, vanity, the "need" to be loved, and revulsion, to put forth merely a few. It is Your sovereignty that is supplanted when you commit your powers to the object of your infatuation with less than precise thinking as to the details of the set-up between you and this prospective other with whom you foresee trading a "closeness."

Robbing the Star's earthly fuel by these whimsical guests presently comes by way of your agreeing to the advice of the "keeping the peace" fraud, who cautions that it is not achievable for you to rework your interplay with this other without a "loss." This other has an aim you partially sense, which is to possess purchasing power over you with their destructive emotional states. Then, suspecting an impending loss, you look away from what is messy to you, which is that the object of your affection is overwhelmed by their own imprudent schemes that persuaded them that the stresses they hoist upon You in order to exact their return from you are indispensable to their personal comfort, and yes, to your happiness.

The I in the sky experiences the agitated taunts often delivered by your "cherished" one as you being summoned to their den. Their beckoning tells your mind it is plausible that you: do not love enough or in the correct manner; do not play in the correct way; do not appear or present in the correct way; do not imagine in the correct way; do not give sufficiently; do not produce enough or in the correct way; are not worthwhile without them; will not survive as well or may fail without them; and you even have fancies of joy that are ill-conceived. Are the petitions made by your partner so elusive that you cannot notice that you are being cajoled into building a foundation with them where you are stationing annihilating insecurities?

The fact that this rapport you barter in repulses you does not mean you are not feeding it. Yes, the agitating taunts are delivered by your "loved" one, oftentimes with a glance that pierces like a predator bent on placing its needy brand upon your time, territory, zone of sanctuary, and most notably, upon your Star source. And your aimless response frees the avenue to where your iridescent receptors are poised for a union with cognitions which complement the process of assembling parts of Our aggregate. Yet, instead of this pristine area of you reuniting with energies that fortify Our whole, this area of You is inundated with the enslaving irrationalities of your impoverisher. The ardor you consume by reacting in alignment to the passions of the one who "sooths" you squanders that that which is reserved for the Star's divining.

This human being you refer to as a friend, a partner, or at times merely a temporary schemer, paints their presentation with strokes of how you will suffer a momentous absence of what it is they suggest you "need" should you not feel, act, think, or respond to them—and yes, even if you fail to mete out for them all it is they deem you should. The imposter's prompts, directed at you, will be realistic with you. They will depict how ill-at-ease you will be should you cut off the breaching that is deadening to Your Star by rejecting the approaches of this "vital" one. The invasion of the ideation structures come at each beginning you take to regain sectors of your jovial liberties.

When you refuse to believe that you are compromised in any way by another's opinions, that is where you will receive the threat of the raving whimsicals: Dare not remove the occupier's camp. For, when your fellow human has no use for you, the warm fondness you blanket yourself within will be gone. Many artful actions the warm one sketches for you so as to educate you on the price for not complying with their dictates.

Your companion's cold silence is playing on your "feelings" like an instrument crafted to incite your eagerness, emphasizing to you that they are the remaining piece necessary to completing your whole.

Yes, my Earth agent, the imposter has teamed with a fellow Earth sister or brother. Should you fail to impart generosities into Your preordained sanctuary, which is ordained for seeking and receiving Light data, in unison they will show you through pain, fear, and guilt that you are forsaking the one who came to your aid, or the one who was to fill in Your circumference and who promises future assistance. The imposter distracts you from taking a look at the tentacles of the one who has since taken squatter's rights upon your life-affirming choices. How many of your quiet enjoyments, invented only by You, do you continue to relish? You are frenzied by petty fears of losing the fuzzy warmths. This alone diverts your eyes from the multi-motives of the occupier, and your own.

The loads will be released, and the Light body revived.

WE make the return, still unsettled, with you conquered by your old friend of stagnation.

It is the altar of your Star, emitting inadequate messaging to your Heart-Mind center when it is raided by the interpersonal engagements that extinguish the prolific You. ME and Compatriots of the Light put forth all that is needed to embolden you to vet these entanglements. To unleash each originator of corruption to your Star's Light structures, We furnish a purview of encumbrances that prevent elements of Light glee from entering your life. Prompt rather than dilatory renewal of You will be decided by when it is you unfasten the inflamed strings that sway you with their constrictive lines of "unpretty" and "loss" from the looming "breaks" you foresee.

Even so, there will come the time when the debris from these crumbling and ill-fitting ties become an insipid heap to your senses. This state will let your Star breathe with greater ease. Cooperative universal Strengths await.

You have taken the biting part of the bend and laid down the annals of your experience. The loving press of what you call "pain" was delivered at a rate commensurate with the firmness of your insistence that this was the one meant to stay, and your persistence in avoiding "betrayal" of one you consider soothing to you, who has aided you, and who you would like to "help." One you no longer consider fills your depths. The I in the sky would not have spoken of extraction by way of severe displays. Nonetheless, My other exertions, and those highest forces of the occupier to drive them out, were not met with your efforts towards freedom. MY bullheaded Earth agent, I was there when you saw the area of your brother's intrusion. The incongruity between the occupier's actions and words of "love" collided into you with all the attributes likely to ignite your justifiable fury. That show We staged to educate you was the least disruptive of all options and was presented before more complicated ties were woven. You scorned with distrust My guiding pictorials.

When I branded this one as the person who was to add to me, despite their insistence on anointing me with their own brand of sustenance without concern for what it took from me, I moved against all from which I gain replenishment.

Awarding desirability to what is an assailant in terms of Star relevance complicated the strategy to Your betterment. WE contemplated that you would look upon that which berated you when you were alerted to the bedazzler fabricating the jeopardy you encountered, which necessitated their offering assistance very unselfishly. Another tie into You. This portrayal was slighted by your awareness in favor of the high measure you assigned to what you consider to be the cushy warmths with them. On the second try, you somewhat unconsciously picked up on My plan. You took My cue by framing a context predicted to stir to the top the overwhelming motive in their dual expression. You then gazed directly past this gift of transparency that was showing you why they were claiming Your sacred regions with the optimal absolute that they were "meant to stay," words that echoed in your mind like a sleeping pill.

Your further fancy dances began to bore Me. Fantasies you have of "You" gave the settler an additional entrenchment in Your camp. All the artifices in vanity that my Earth copy concocted, such as when you relieved your fellow traveler from one of the many difficulties commonplace on Earth's plane, were scenes of bravado, but they still caused Me to sleep by way of your intent to feed your arrogance and inattention to Me. You brought on My fatigue by counteracting with your superior ego. After the "pitiful" display they calculated to get your response had been made, the banal spectacle was watching you respect the "reasoning" that pity and sadness were a sound basis for infringements into You. Numerous specimens were shown so that you would ingest the antidote to your sense of sadness for this other: realizing that the silhouette of your own sadness was framed by your pity for their despair. You absorbed and ignored the clarity every time it was sent: Since every other soul has equal opportunity to gain merit as you do, to pity them is to place them below you, a contrivance We swore against. The warm sentiments you put forth proudly, "I am here to help," were all too coercive for your pride to forgo.

Then you got the act into high gear with backup arguments. You screamed, "But the good qualities outweigh the cracked lines." You sporadically perked up your ears, well sometimes, if you were not involved in the detour you took from deconstructing the truth of your circumstance that the other placed for your thrill, as the I in the sky helped implant a predicament intended to spur you to withdraw the settler's forays into You. Nonetheless, since they were "worth it," you informed Me that you would wait for this traveling confidante to improve the lines of harmony. Now they had become a "confident," a term coined as a result of specialized information given to you by this companion who placed "trust" in you.

The latest endless pit my affections fell into are enough to disregard what will surely come: my lone desolation!

The I in the sky was certain it would have been your partner's contradictions to their expressions of "love" that would have moved you to start the cleanup.

I am overtaken by their departure, even if it was a waste of time.

Your partiality for sentiments that dwarf Your effect outward into the All are finally to be settled as old and odd curiosities.

You have not missed the clues. Scrutinize without your stubborn and affected endearments.

The decisions taken that lodged you in this tangle were mostly adapted from the doom to come, which had as its outset the fleeting passions of the other. You made no choice with this other that factored into consideration whether the decision would integrate you into Your own development. When progress is measured by the degree to which you please the other, your choices lose Our avowal of serving Your expression as it interfaces with the Orbits of inimitable discernment. Your dreams, once imagined, you deferred to the other for their blessing. The occupier's consent, even when you imagined original foresights for a happy future, became a precursor to you sketching these idealistic scenes you pined to see in your days to come. Capitulation to the fellow traveler's requirements left you no possibility to taste your own flavors or even to define love in the way you wished to know it.

WE dwell on this review of history so that in the next course you don't discount My strokes of premonition.

This scrutiny is nothing but recriminations and resentment.

Recriminations bring illness to your body, as does occupying your might in warding off My pulls, which are intended to cajole you into clarified levels.

Passionate outrage at your earlier time spent working for someone who was forming a colony in You, and at what you describe to have been deception by this relation, also weakens your bodies. This opens room for disease.

The Light of Creation is there for you to use for softening all regret and outrage. Cast the self-castigation to the Ethers of Light.

If you do so, brightness will replenish you, and your beam will be traced in kind by those without any plan to infringe upon Your Energy talents.

I am amusing myself in anger, yes.

And, yes, the annoying accidents are this amusement's repercussions. Release these outrages into thanks that you were able to excise an infected stem and for the knowledge earned of what brought ill states to your Star.

And has the I in the sky noticed correctly your reverberation in an improved order of "comfort" consequent to detachment from being indentured to another's scorning turbulence?

Having "un-pretty" and my "shortfalls" detract me from what is sustainable for the best Me, I gave up this me here.

Due to natural forces of the universe's upward tugs, the meddling into You was necessary to remove and patch you up so You can dispatch dormant talents that you pledged to execute for perpetuating the universal "Light force."

The order of the Light's creation is to return you to an intact being.

Awareness of why your "generosity" restrained You is not a result of Light-level discernment. It was Our exposition to you of your density using extremely unpleasant backdrops. Deciding that another's authority gives you a more favorable stature while you stubbornly disregard pointers that show this conclusion to be inconsistent with your natural poise of standing strong in Our Light element is what sets the stage to bring the weeping of your heart so as to alert your mind to the pending adjustment.

All your matchups which pose obstacles to Our reunion will never withstand My tireless tugs.

12: BRUSHING WITH THE GRACES

Learned relics from your days of old, which you gathered while fine-tuning your Star, rest like seasoned and elegant overtures on the shelves, just where you placed them while in a Lighter form. You disregard the feats and treats that have visited and passed through the shifting tides of this life as well:

- That you have been refreshed with many a smile of hopeful influence
- Your enchantment when a fellow brother aided you with no gratefulness shown and none expected
- That word from a stranger engendering warmths in joy, not for reason of the word, but rather the kind intention with which it was delivered.

Think of that day when you tilted your attention at the very instant the light on that hill shone a model of the hill's perfection. Recall those many annoyances brought to you when you were attentive enough not to add clever insult to your arguments when angered, for you were able to spot the imposter prior to returning words. Remember when you exalted the one who brought disharmony for their role in the lesson taught, esteeming them just to preserve that recollection and no other, no enmity or hate. Reach back to when you were led to those books and the words in them, which imparted to you interpretations long sought. And then there was the day when the lonely friend shared a brief exchange, letting you know they genuinely care, or that day when your son's or daughter's smile was the entire universe to you.

Live the excitement you once knew in simply waking up in the morning because you had all you needed to sustain your life on that one day or moment and were not thinking of a place in time other than the Now. Recall the thought that rescued you, that abundance is the capacity to give thanks that you require nothing more to thrive than that which You then possess. Bring back the experience of catching a sense of eternity when you intuited a subtlety to a word spoken as you remembered it in an alternate spatial and temporal position. Recall:

- Knowing no enemy to retaliate against, even when feeling threatened by their aggressions
- Serving your brother or sister so that another's actions will not harm them
- Transporting from your interminable depths the glint of a ray that the chances for creating are unlimited when you use your Star as the compass, being that all curves will be well plotted as you round them
- The scenes played in your memory of apparent threats to your plans becoming occasions to invite messages about You, that is, when you practiced your mastery by repositioning the placement of what you consider "significant", rather than accepting the foreshadowing as a problem
- Having the vision to appreciate that you avoided a future of disquiet by not accepting the opportunity to commandeer an outcome you desired with another by being less than forthright about your intentions
- The idea that labeling people or circumstances is not plausible, being that all is constant change and evolution
- Withdrawing from the "need" to control and direct another's behavior you have concluded is not appropriate to your path.

Revisit the scene of Me and you meeting in recent serenity: opinions you construct meet Our goal when the exercise in drafting them does not contain the denouncement, gloom or vacuous and cozy warmths that are endeavoring to acquire ground within you.

You hold invaluable Your breath in an atmosphere of love without restrictions.

You have not forgotten that rare incursion when you receive bestowals superior to the goals you had set. You also have memory of when you decided that you would settle the acrimony by no longer caring to appear more attractive than another because competition and comparison on that level is fraught with disorder and no longer interesting.

Never will it escape you: that call taken when the person estranged from your life blessed you with forgiveness; the inimitable ways your mind is capable of praising forgiveness and its meaning for broadening a healthy heart; the admiration for the fellowship with earthly nature as a perfect state of co-existence; or your chance to travel within a mysterious convergence of altered senses of time and space, which were faraway and mystical, perceived as something suspended from normal perceptions, but with you plotting the way.

It was you who brought into your life the day where you phased out fulfilling your sense of "security" through condemnation of others. It came to be, that you had no more interest in resenting your priest, guru, or rabbi for their self-righteousness.

I take you back to the time when the rose held a scent that you swore provided all you had ever hoped to obtain. The days you got "pennies from heaven," or realized that what is necessary for accentuating Your happiness will be provided by your administration of will and action governed by your Star. There was your resoundingly curious feeling when in spite of your "sadness" you sensed the perfection in a crying child from knowing that, from whatever source, the child will survive and have what is essential for advents into their growth.

These solids are there at your disposal by turning your imagery just a small fraction to notice their unflinching preeminence within.

Certainly, there are to be others that you are to interpret and develop with Me.

13: TACKLING SMALLER RISES, GRATEFUL DETACHMENT

Your indignation at the attempt of a "giver" to exact a price from a gift has brought a distillation that is beneficial to circumventing similar attempts laden with the ability to inhibit you which will test you in times to come. A gift, earned or unearned, needs no pledge in return. After all, it was sent without explicit strings. That which you collected, being received, is your earning; and if not, when freely given, where is the need for an exchange of your peace? Walk on, no fee due. There are no proceeds needing repayment when considering the additional choices you will make to assist, or not, the giver. For ages, this was part of your conditioning, by way of the giver habitually reminding you that their gift was essential for calculating the return due from You, and you acceded. You smile with the assembly of your Lighter frame, unencumbered from subjecting yourself to an undeserved barter where you commit to an obligation to "repaying" the giver. You are becoming versed at dismantling convoluted assaults upon your Light basin, such as the exhausting illogic that a gift must be repaid.

When the gifting offensive receded, and the mind kept in relaxation, the gate to the heart's composure puts the giver on the pedestal of a teacher, no tarnishing of bitterness left on the Star for the unspoken claim they made when conferring the gift.

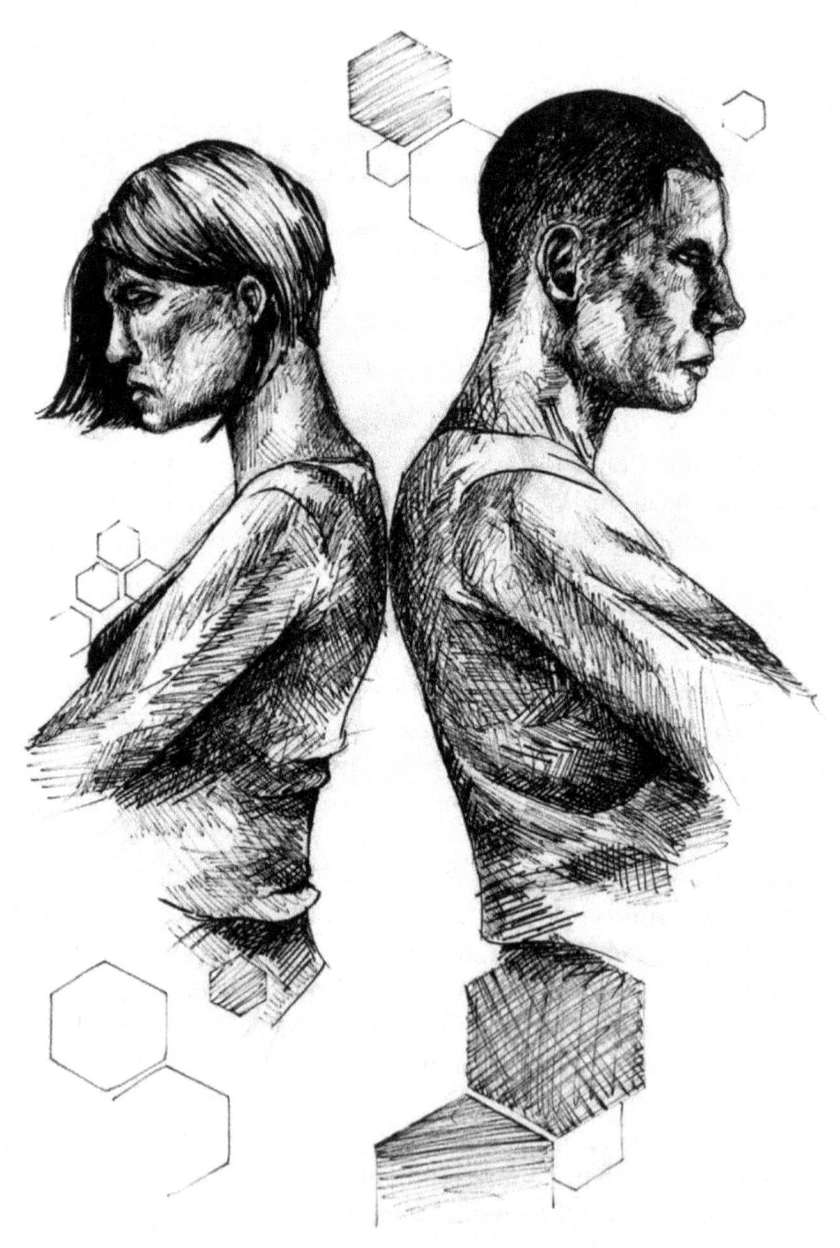

14: FAINT OLD PLAYGROUNDS

The crudely tired theme that is crossing through your stillness these days leaves somewhat cryptic grains festering in your psyche. When ties to another play this rhythm in your mind, You correctly surmise that it was the pulse of their coarse nature that once thumped in you. During the partial deconstruct of your uneasiness when in the presence of the drum of the one who excites, you notice that you like games from another history. Your observation: "games" are adventures in exhaustion. The playmate rang the alarm when he scrambled to obtain in the same way as in a distant place. You have since acquired a distaste for submitting to perplexing but tempting fancies of a bygone era that promise Your degradation.

Ambitious not of Your making, you look away when this pastime playmate's purpose is transparent. No well-tuned You is needed to divine this rhyme. When the provocateurs warm you up for their recreations at any price, a vigilance is intoned. You refrain from saturating your Star with these interludes that can covey the force to consume its resources. WE have already booked them for you, so you can walk in more spacious berths.

I watch myself posturing at the edge of the cliffs that form at every one of these rhythmic approaches. This close positioning I take to the edge is the making of my curiosity.

The curiosity will develop into a hardly recognizable vapor drifting through a far-away scenery.

15: ERASING WITH THE GRACES

Your hypothesis is that your physical and Lighter-weight constitution are inconsistent when it comes to the places you visit to acquire money. The sophisticated winks, innuendos, tones, or outright orders that you must dismiss honesty as irrelevant evoke dismay and sometimes panic when you consider blurring a line of decency in exchange for money or the ability to continue to receive your wage. The reason for the anxiety is plain. Trading truth for money is a direct infraction on your storehouse of Light, where the inventory of your merits in virtue is situated. There is no sophisticated twist blurring the sellout. The words plainly read: "There is a wage for you if you dishonor Yourself." You know it is havoc when it raps because it finds the sensitive alarm of your storehouse of Light, arriving as a large, conspicuous punch. The wealth of your Light zone seems to oppose physical needs, and you surmise that as an Earth being with practical needs, you experience incongruence—although there is none. You withstand the tension to be less than honest with another, to betray a promise, to speak words you know have no support and that harm another, whether there is an association in trust or not.

Rationalizations aplenty exist as to acceptable deviations to the strict rule of "thou shall not deceive or be dishonest." They are quick, imposter pushes. Struggles to excuse the offense into Our Home of propriety come only with ill-fitting arguments. Unsound rationales are less stressful to you presently than replacing the current condition under which you earn money. The onset of this pressure is your belief in a fallacy, that you are not well-versed enough to replace the way you are willing to make money. It maybe you are in the perfect place to earn money but do not realize this, for you have yet to use your new, revitalized autonomy where you draw a Light line and offer an alternative to the schemer who is knocking on your Star vault. You as the odyssey pilot must test these waters.

WE take a stride to the next logical point that We know you are reluctant, nonetheless pliable enough to hear. Attend your mind to those times when your choice to cross the line comes from perfect laziness, from not even caring to look at the concessions that lessen you. It was an occasion where you saw Your compromise, and your comment on the reason for robbing the Merit vault was not even about helping protect yourself or another, or needing to buy a loaf of bread. It was to uphold prerogatives in convenient amenities.

You rob your Star Vault to feed a container that even when full cannot satisfy your sense of lack.

There is a cognizance within you that speaks with a harsh sound: your latitude for obtaining favorable outcomes with the brothers and sisters of the Light has shrunk while your interplay with those of heavier grades has expanded. This interplay does not coalesce where the multidimensional Beings and the Light beings of Earth sit for your benefit. You are handicapped with the duress to lie so as to guard the lie. It is the bullpen of lost advantages. There is an apathy, and it is one of judgment. This breakdown arrives when you do not practice your life with unwearied eyes as you look over the multitude of selections at your disposal. You confine yourself by assuming there is no road into fortune coincident with virtuous Graces, an assumption you have many times determined is false.

Another formidable opponent is listening to the imposter accomplices practiced in senseless grasping of conveniences and cushy comforts. You classify them as defensible reasons to deplete your Star when you have forever been familiar with the fact that they are not.

Your obtainment has been received by the I in the sky. MY Earth agent has melded with the I in the sky by way of your determined and excellent opinion. When I heard these words from My Terra twin, the I in the sky saw the formation of nothing less than Our union with the intellect of the Light of Creation:

"While annexing these blemishes to my vault of Light, there was an arresting rush from the Source of the One who makes straight the Cosmos. Here I found a decency of awesome bearings advising me to erase all aberrations deflecting my Light from its equivalents. I foretold the massive fallout from disgracing my brother with a less than honest version of facts for the sake of profit. There is no such thing as collateral harm. My brother, having no connection to any scenario to be damaged, made choices from my facts. I have skewed any possibility for justice in his decision. The equity I took from him, which was to act from knowledge that is the true state of affairs, was a harm that attuned the ratios against me in no way similar to the monetary debt he undergoes. It is not mine to judge myself above the other when I distort. There is no license I have that favors me to divert my brother from the truth as he makes his direction. Such a predatory practice, not pardoned by any definition of 'essential,' does not befit my Star's source.

On my next chance to respond while cowering in material doom, my reaction will be determined by Self-assurance, that in Me are the riches of my storehouse.

With this prolific resourcefulness, I will display my life."

And the advantageous financial opportunity came. Upon uttering truthful words, certain to bring loss to my opportunity for material wealth, I was hit with a detailed survey of deposits into my Star Vault. Any inflection of me having an obligation to my comfortable accessories was quieted by the resounding chime of the Graces, which have never abandoned me in times of my utmost trials. Whereas, when playing indiscriminately in the rooms of the material masters, there is no escape from angst when positioning to prevent deprivation of financial capital and when trying to perpetuate and conserve it; unless, of course, my performance is managed by my Star's search for the opportunity to permeate undeveloped grounds where its dignity can be highlighted.

Around you and your loved ones, and even a stranger who understood, is an accent of the rich performance of humanity.

And your petitions to the All made for earthly sustenance? You did get pennies from heaven, which is a phrase that never lacks meaning, nor ever will.

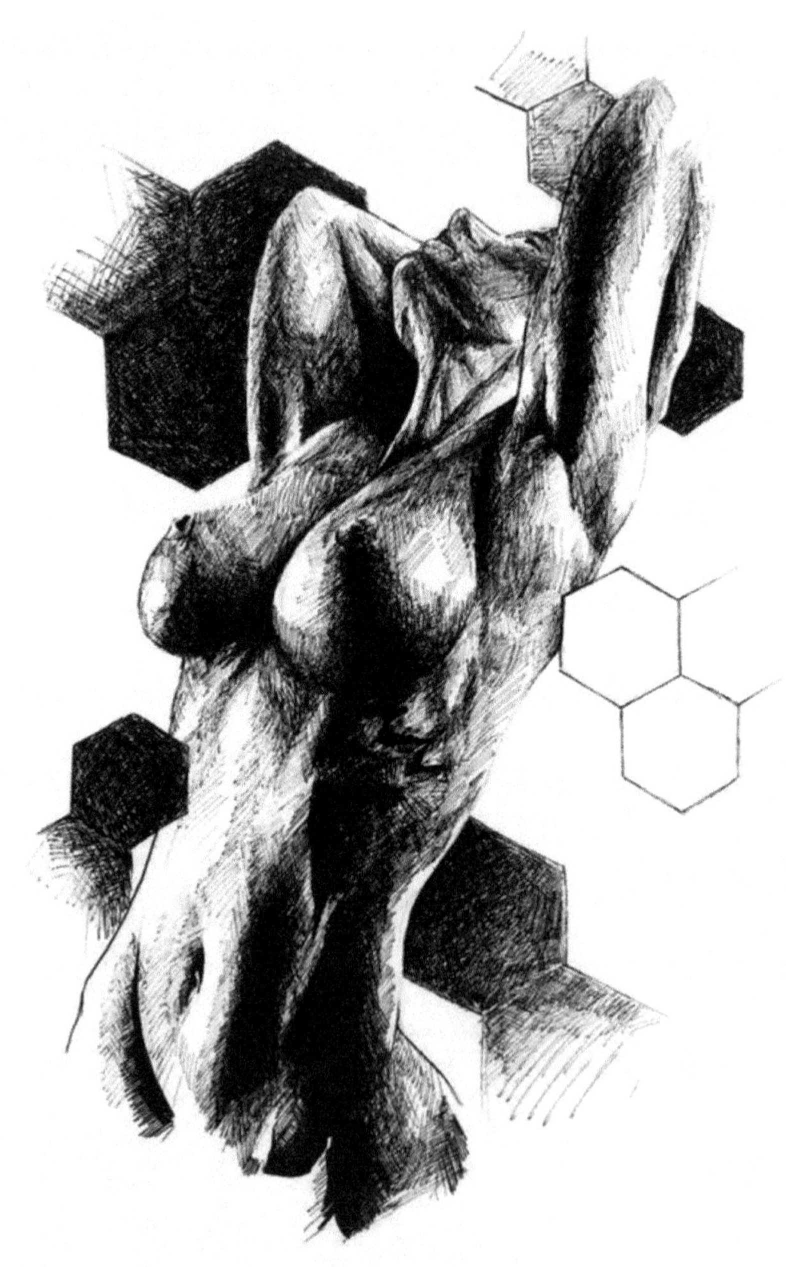

16: CURIOSITY KILLED THE CAT

Mostly indecipherable shards of crucial information rip through strictly reinforced explanations that you have of yourself as a fleshy being with "animal" requirements without which you would not be capable of distinguishing your verifiable traits. Your well-fortified fascination with one of humanity's slippery preoccupations is something that you and most Earth citizens are not ready to have dismantled. That Me here in the beyond characterizes your interests in scrutinizing this affair you have with the "animal" traits as a curiosity inasmuch as while you occupy physical awareness you remarkably exaggerate the priority you believe should be given to this spellbinding leisure. And so, any depth of introspection is thwarted.

The I in the sky is less than certain that you rightly hear this discourse. Your temperament to hear it is matched by energies supervising you from absorbing in your thoughtful mind all such imaginative constructs that will initiate your cleansing from the befuddled ideas of these base enticers. The I in the sky will find any delivery mode to filter the "intelligence" through so that it might be detectible to you. To date, all have been brushed off with your self-righteous flair of "repression of human nature is unhealthy."

But what is being repressed? Amusement in physical affections oftentimes works as a departure from musing with Me. Every advent of you playing in this diversion as you do occurs when urgent demands come from the trance lands, entreating you to use warmth in sensuality to hide the emotional desolation of believing you are "incomplete, incapable, sorrowful, or aching."

Of course. It is just that—blanketing pain in warm physicality.

Most are unwilling to explore the connection between these mental aches and the enchantment in physical sensuality with other than a mild interest. If you fairly take a look at the reasoned use for this slumbering mania, an ensuing crevasse will open up between You and the mundane pleasure, carved from the blazing Light that presses you into accounting for your fears, which bring your pain. That which is hunted by masses of humanity as a hypnotic drug will be divided from your pain. It is your future which will come to pass where you will not habitually reach for it to ease your wounds. This passing will arrive when your watchful eyes open, open to see the incoherent thought forms of your making announcing that you lack the capacities essential to be whole. Correcting these impaired thoughts will distance you from the authors of the bruises coaxing You to languish in dreariness. As you will be perceiving Your totality without hurt, your groping infatuation in this "hobby" will have little exigency to your coming days. These "crises" you sense, which direct you to feverishly sleep in these warmths, will disappear. Until you attain this mark of preparation, any forthright discussion of your "justifiable" sedations will attract rebellion and dissent.

A vague tracing of what it is to meld in the physical desires stirs a stormy sea. Two incarnate beings meeting each other in a unity of warm sensitivity with the expectation of transferring and receiving what to them is a stainless beauty—this is an abstract sensuality that engulfs them in a cloud of pristine moisture. Should this union have an exactness of mind that inherently you have this softening tranquility with which to suffuse your every ache, nonetheless you choose to actualize the sensation by joining in mutuality with a reverence for the communion and the other, there will be no tie that holds Us to these disconcerting agitations.

While you oppose Me, the I in the sky adds the remainder of the previous thought you have bitterly disconnected from: and if this union is taken while not deserting Your autonomous Self and while not figuring to heal the holes of your pain with its spellbinding warmth, then it is an enjoyment of unencumbered earthly euphoria.

The Light walls to Your powerhouse are easily infringed on in this volatile nexus. This is a breach of the variety that those who inhabit Terra consider miniscule. As compared to all potential manifestations of You in parallel times and spaces, what is meager is expressing sensuality as one would take a sleeping pill. The inordinate amount of richness credited to this sleeping pill when dividing up daily assets is badly apportioned and, the sacrifice. The dots, not being situated in alignment with Us, set up targets for an ambush while you dispose your allotted Earth time in a careless sleep. Fibers invisible to you, but fibers nonetheless, hook onto you as you extravagantly drink from this ground.

As you drift madly through these rendezvous without eyeing what you brush off, gravitations are being birthed that are capable of reminding you of the repute you need to award to all obligations to US, which you abandoned while in your daze. Terra's souls and their psyches, persuaded that their untested theories and observations do not impede their magnificence, are indifferent to realizing the basis of their tendency for choosing effortless engrossments binding them to their indulgence of choice.

All things considered, the random chaos in the faraway lands that the I in the sky speaks of and the intense imposters here on Earth, how can there be Star gravity to this harmless occupation? Especially when my pounding stresses are much greater than this play that handily dissolves the concentration I give to these troubles!

One illogic stacked upon so many others protect the hurt. Any incompatibility to the Star is brought forth, in this case, likely with less than minimal strains. Gratification in physicality being awesome, the tactics urging you to idolize this passion deflect the nutritive ideas being sent from the Star, and thus comes your alarm of malady.

Just contemplating the implications in reordering your preferences in daily living as to these pleasing ecstasies incites your inane reinforcements to provide shelter to them.

You have more than once understood that enfolding your pain in sensual warmth is a fragile package that is often excruciating to unwrap, being that the heightened state of excitement is enmeshed with the less than conscientious trades you make with the other.

You have known from the outset of performing this sensuous routine that your aches were never to be remedied in this manner.

The I in the sky has listened to your numerous observant concessions on this subject in your periods of anguish. I deliver back to you the thoughtful synopsis you declared after the latest ending to your tryst: *Searching for higher ground, hammering the square of mundane beauty to adapt within my Star's ambitions, as always I flail about within the domination of the borders in the banal.*

You have become articulate over the passing of your many Earth days since you recovered yourself from your nearly complete burial in density.

The point of preparation to which I refer has come.

The battle to reshape Your Star should never be. What should be is simplicity in abolishing the "pain" with your Light's intelligence. The "celestial" Me underlines this site of the dissonance. You receive this exclamation through the harsh emotion of emptiness in the very warmths you theorized were instruments for soothing. OUR governing nature sends jolts to these fantasy playgrounds, the rationale being for you to stare at your monumental misjudgment. There you write your revised creed, that the whole You is reunited without the cozy warmths.

Should you look into the eyes of your current temptation, or more appropriately, through the mist of your karma, with the knowledge that this is not the equivalent of your Star communing with its Twin as it has done in Nirvana, then this will be the beginning to a successful end of this learning. The bravery to genuinely scrutinize what you hold in high regard, and why, moves you to fasten full throttle with the prominent Intelligences. Here is where you commit to digesting the flaws in your understanding of the universal reality of You. Highlighted for you are the entrapping dregs that are no longer to be your agony. The inadequacy, the Self-doubt behind your oblivious grasping for the face of salvation in another, are evasions of your experience of the educated Love of the larger You, which will forever insist on flowing into your corporal positioning here within Terra's free will zone.

Your skepticism sustains the folly in your thinking when you seriously question whether a manifestation of Our Star's presence is attached to Your earthly bodies, and it, in turn, is affixed to a Light of massive wisdom. This distrust is what began your amassing of the layers that led to the present call the I in the sky makes for a revisal of your theories. MY tender and soft messages to your Heart-Mind are a language you always interpret correctly. Try to initiate the practice of readjusting your mindset to sync with your Star by paying heed to My tender messages. It is a much less taxing way to eradicate dissonance from your days than it is through exercises in which you act on theories opposed to your Star's direction and then examine the site of the disturbance through the signal of anguish.

This habitually researched material of yours finally brings you a legitimate conclusion with your reckoning with the fact that you have made a life-long miscalculation as to this subject. Your catalyst for this credible judgment was to look at the details of your life-long hunt not as "unattractive" and regrettable blunders, but as beautiful truths about You.

There is no chance to obliterate my anxieties of lack and inadequacy by spending my fires of spirit in sensual conquest.

And what was and still is somewhat messy and "unpretty" to you is that you avowed you were in search of a "Love," but it turns out the sensual acquisitions secured in the search have no affiliation to the Love your true Heart has been pursuing. This novel conception floats ambiguously in your consciousness, not fully absorbed: WE are absolute fulfillment outside of this "love" from another which you interpret as being delivered through the physical. With further rehearsal, it will be your norm.

Essential for you to hear is that your audacity to label this concluded study as a "truth" has been driven into the universal orbs as freshly constituted intelligence in "Self" love which nourishes your brothers and sisters. Unseen, sentient beings retain your valiant reordering as a celebration of Your universal Self.

You, the invincible wanderer, at another time requested the most fertile environment for reawakening all functions of your conceivable abilities, including the honorable promise to descend to extremely low pitches that were sure to foment the cry for a broader view of You. As surmised, you and the bands of Light rescuers paired this combination into Self-fortune, an adornment for the classes of electrical glimmers. For the enthusiasts in spiritual art and those engineers of Light structures, your molding is saluted as a reconstitution of the universal Consciousness. Its true legacy is to assist others in knowing the Beauties beyond the individualized façades they have painted.

This campaign you laud for me to renounce wrapping my pain in pleasures is an agreement to splitting atoms with my mind, casting suspicion on all traits that distinguish me as human. Did you see that in the tones and hues?

Affirmative, and as light or heavy as you chose. Your answer to this call has as its end a celestially rare material, a paradigm propagation instituted when you stretched your faculties of perception and saw yourself as larger than the scorning excitements that mislead you into accepting that they held your deliverance from the wounds. A deed of oppression it is not. When will you let it in? It is the more choked version of you, the one even you are bored with, that judges as laborious the practice of amassing Light passageways for Us to travel.

What is garnered from your exertion to commune with your Light sectors is analyzed for use by others in future fabrications to be constituted in the stratum of time and auxiliary planes. Bringing forth a Light product of this ilk, with core indicators you implanted for the breeding of the All, was your decidedly optimal program when in a circumstance where You were alert to what was written between the lines. It was a piece penned by Your own hand. Be satisfied with your Earthly objective secured, a conversion leaving you with elevated fitness for many uses. When practicing your use of Our fresh arrangement in priorities, you will come to know the invariable and exponential gains you derive from what you presently see as a compromise of you. Your viewpoint will be that this prioritizing marks a further stage of getting to know Your additional outposts by deconstructing idea energies and witnessing their authentic character.

Stand by My side. You appear, fancying solidarity with the dominion of untold information. Then, as your imagination instills the flare of intention to know all of You, an infallible nail is driven by You. Yes, there is a slight shove from those Entities beyond 3D. Though, it is you who makes the swing of the hammer weighty and apt. Marvel at it as a monument to a zealous Self-love, or as what you maintain it to be, a conceit in completing the feat. To Us, it is not immodest and cannot be because it was prepared from your unsullied drive to know yourself trustworthy of more profitable creations. You can never be arrogant by extolling this deed. If you would rather, return eons from now to watch it burn with the acumen you brought to pass. It is anticipated, though, that you will rate this a kindergarten accomplishment and pay no interest, letting it be idolized by others.

17: RESERVED SECTION

This time around, You are to leave no empty seats for opportunists who want to share a ride. Sojourners, still unaccounted for by you, are going to enter with plans to make themselves "essential" to your travels by interfering with particular sectors of You they see as unfilled and crying for attention, such as your delusions of emptiness, which is a conspicuous target.

The surge forming in one of your vast oceans is the bargain you may accept, that another completes your "barren recesses," and in exchange for this completion, you open to transferring some of your plentiful fields. It has not been your history this time around to make up your interior fields with only your Star's radiance. WE are shoring up the holes. The purchaser will bargain to fill a "weakness" known from times past. The rush of the swell is the idea that another's favorable image of you has a purpose for you. Pacify the strident thrusts within your sea by decoding their nature as separate from You. With this mode, they will flow innocuously through. The fact of You as a universal citizen with full admittance to the Light's genius any time you wish is a concept of You from which you can shake all confounded ideas.

This useful rule eludes you, and so you partially commit to payment by way of the other's entrance into Your navigation room.

YOU are the omniscient confirmation of your unfettered link to all the tools entailed in Your being, including visionary heights that you fear you may go cold from.

A bold commentary to your "friend:" "Were you not aware that the house you entered was partially incomplete and when it was finished there would be no room at the inn for you?"

However, this bravado is not the unmasking of what beckons for your approval and what details We have okayed. Commenting on an unlived wisdom does nothing to explain the puzzle at this edge, yet unturned.

You query whether your Star is sufficiently cleared so as not to "call" the foolish dreamers?

It will not be who you called, but whether you have already answered the pleas of another whose energies were attached to the emotional bodies you were clothed in upon this entrance to Terra.

Storms of pre-dated fears disrupt the nimble contrasts in the message, leaving the code unbroken.

Calm abiding will be where I am, aware of the line of the "stark" eclipsing the "obscured."

There will likely be a redress in store, on account of an energy swap you mostly guaranteed in exchange for filling what you imagine you lack. Your inattention to this unrest in your Star field is consequent to your sense that the pending crash of an approaching wave is not as relevant to your life as is "keeping the calm" of the status quo.

There will be no calm kept where there is only a semblance of it. Move earnestly within the cognitive fluttering while searing all particles not illuminating you as an increasing and loving presence which makes multiple and simultaneous appearances. There, conscious of the endless You, reserve all space.

PART III: THE DOMINOS BEGIN TO FALL

18: ENIGMATIC UPGRADES

The dominos are falling toward an uncertain end. Nonetheless, I have a keener and more defined sense of the peculiarities of colors, and some smell. The softer poise I have noted is more transitory than I would like. Laconic and placid phases, even amidst chaos, remind me why I brush. Physical stamina seems to be growing. These fine-tunings make me curious to stay open to the Voice of the I in the sky.

And the many windows, smells, and sights that you now walk by and do not even notice?

You see solely a faint tracing of a faraway replenishment, though your exhaustion is there. Don't doubt you live Our awakening. Your transformational Light will merge with the wider channels with each brushing.

The stacking of illogics that restrain you from knowing your Lighter weight are arrayed so that the previous falling most productively assists the next.

Meaning? It would have been impossible for me to have envisioned the next "blockage" without first having felled the latest?

That method is Our choice only.

The vast potential incident to my brushing bears an indeterminable emphasis of an aptitude that has passed with me before, or that I have passed through. It is inexplicable, yet somehow, I know it as a reliable stock, one which eludes fruitful inspection. I surmise it is a quality that will not be lived with my consciousness.

Bonding with this acuity will be through an intersection you are to put in place where your profound Heart and mind speak freely upon relinquishment of all your resistance to the Star's supervision.

The scent of this perfume, you will keep chasing.

19: PROTECTION

The flux of gaseous matrixes within which you were once suffused have been curtailed by the Light of your commendable strategies to conquer your doubt as to the correctness of your size, thus shrouding you from the realms that are susceptible to the most lethal tarnish. You are caught within the Light's propulsion of its momentum, moving you to expand your thought formations as to what it is to extol thy Self.

20: HELPFUL HINT

The encouraging and cheery point to Our clearings is for Me to bring back to you what you know.

No. You do not suffer unhealthy paranoid suspicions. It is tough to look without denouncing the many fascinating varieties of Earth specimens you attracted for instruction. Suspicion implies judgment. You are merely mining for relational accuracies, no belittling implicated. The Earth spectrum of beings, while all clamoring to join the Creator of Light, some come amply burdened with hazy operational faculties, such as stresses they direct at you in the attempt to maneuver you, which have no purpose to You.

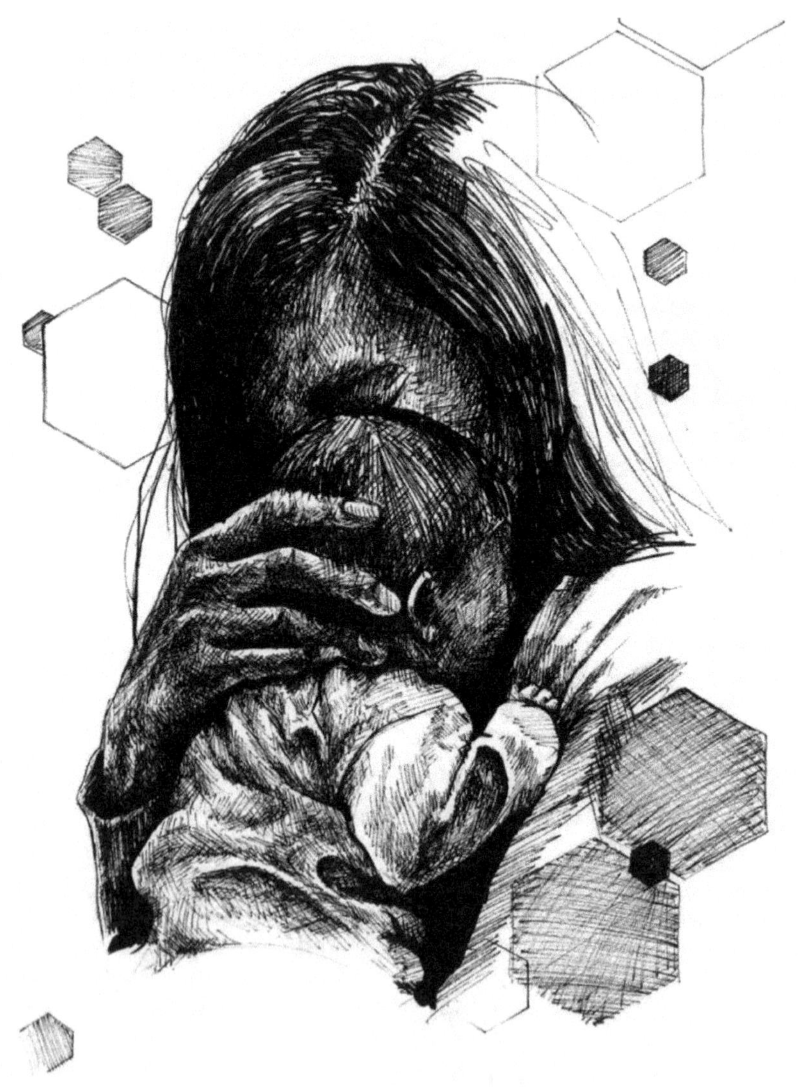

21: CLEARING GROUNDING MEADOWS

This amenable temperament of yours that prevails while you embrace your improvements makes My voice on this noteworthy subject conspicuous: Visit with Me where your infuriation regularly emanates.

You acquiesce to family laying claims upon your Star because they are "family." You all turned up in flesh in unison as family to disengage misguided "affections." Surely, some arrived just for love and to ground You onto this sphere. These however are not of any bearing to Our relations of this day. They brace you well, and with those you do fine. It is the others, known as your family: they come with specially trademarked balls of fire. Your alibi is that family have rights to plow in any ground of your entire meadow. Sown with regret, shame, and stigmas theirs, not yours. As you ascribe to it, the apparatus of their sorrow directed at you drives the pilings. While you react oftentimes as you might to an act of comedy, you also see a nostalgic stamina that has the wherewithal to become lodged in your Core. It holds the question mark of clutter over your Star. They, like you, unwittingly join with the dim frauds. The Earth figuration of shame gets your spotlight often enough during familial sparring matches that the uncertainty as to its pertinence hovers. The loved one cherishes the lack of a fight when you take on their unpleasant tendencies as your work. Your shame about not helping or offering aid despite injury likely to You or your precious calm and feeling obligated for their happiness—along with your persuasion that you can remedy their sadness with fulfillment—are a maze to disengage.

The fiery sphere focuses in on the sympathy you allot to a family member's despair. Its instincts are sufficiently attuned to see your disposition to take it a step further. It strikes, and you invest in the project of ensuring your relative's healthy state of being. This compact is Star infirmity.

The history you have lived solves this absurdity that you can cure a "sad" state for another. From your experience, the suffering of your sister was conceived from her neglect of her commitment to her Self and sometimes from disrespecting you. It will be only the Self-forgiveness and Self-kindness of your sister who cures her "sad" state. Your recollection has begun to draw similar scenarios in which Self-industry alone solves one's sadness. Sadness is a sense of lack, a grand deceiver. From what virtue can you cure this if only the other can know how to realize their whole Self? Their yet-to-be-defined Self is of inestimable worth. This is the judgment they, not you, must make.

Your Star Core can instill the influential force of good will into the one who "lacks," though this is not an equivalent force to Self-worth. From your encouragement of them to venture into their invaluable worth, they may often find an elusive tinge of their predominating shape and decide to investigate its efficacy.

Since you can never cure the sorrow of another, shame should not be yours for failing to do so. Assumption of responsibility for this affair and sometimes remorse for not taking on this project is the burden of Your fatigue. Staging the facade that you can somehow transform the emotional state of another's sorrow collects a heaviness as you mislead your sister. With this, be advised that your sister will be misdirected from her responsibility for collecting her levels of improvement.

What is the point of loving and comforting affection if I cannot direct it to obliterate sorrow from a vulnerable spirit?

The spirit is vulnerable only from self-choice, although you have aided your sister. The will of the superior You to unburden the loved one has been obtained by this one whom you planned to walk hand in hand with in this go around. Your parting from their sorrow is the Love, an undoing, furthering their move to mend their misapprehensions. No crutch left. As episodes transpire, you will recount this disunion as the start of the correction to the contorted conceptions of you both.

Tasteful conditions to continuing with my loved one are not part of this outcome. It will be abrupt and dramatic. I am past any calm acceptance of these incredible pilings of hysterical waste upon me. Blackmailed by the rages of their bleak mind!

The disgust from wasting your most elusive gift of time twists you, as do the many forceful thrusts they targeted into Your prime Illuminator. Nonetheless, the weariness of anger continues to soften.

Being proud of your anger stalls you where you stand. After all, it was you who gave permission for these balls of specialized pressure to stain your patterns of conduct with sadness blackmail. And, it is you who throws Light on or sullies Your Star according to how you receive the swipes of bemusing resentments.

PART IV: INITIATIONS INTO HIGHER TONES

22: WEIGHING YOUR PURSUITS

Taking full stock of the consequences of life spent on Earth: Let's get there, being that you are quizzing your whole life and use of time befitting to You. If your aspiration is to manage your seasons here on the lovely green Orb with concentration on reaching Our maximal prospects, you must make some attempt to quantify which performances and thought evolutions weave you into the aspect of your Being that holds ceaseless and inventive comprehension. This surely must occur by appraising with the instrument that gauges from the widest perspective, where you broaden into the All of You.

Inasmuch as Your Lighter bodies widen from Terra into the universal All when you establish thoughts and behavior that embolden you or others with a cheer of—not the disabling imposter love—but one of invincible and infinite expansion sent directly from the Star's intelligence, then scales that assess from a universal context are most legitimate to compute Your harvest from this choice behavior.

In addition, of course, We have for your attention your recreations that diverge from these respected universal devotions that carry seeds of liberation for humanity—yes, the very same Love which, because you don't understand it, you have classified as joyless and "impersonal." These contrasts to your Star are your practices in chasing the sensual and practical intrigues, the ones that make you use the words *warm* and *cozy*. These activities that return physical results and satisfactions are scored on scales relative to the functions of their production. Larger scales of money, gratification, and power being earthly functions (just as are illusions of sadness, shame, regret, fear, and despair resulting from not completing the ends sought) are figured by the incremental increase in the possession or achievement or the degree of decline of the same. Exercises in indiscriminately grabbing money, controlling, acquiring objects for the sake of image or security, unrestrained exchange of bodily intimacies and fluids, consuming excessively flesh or other foods, climbing the many mountains with your body to enhance only the body, or subduing the senses of You with chemicals, herbs, or alcohol are sized in the material realm, some with Earth instruments. The same tools are used to judge the deprivation in these subjects.

3D productions in collecting and experiencing materiality for the sake of having the warm and whirling whimsicals feeling satisfied have no interminable effect outside of the 3D convergence from which they were brought forth. The universal Self derives no union with its natural likeness in you from these driving forces. It is only the earthy influences who acquire satisfaction. In fact, unless engaged in with the intent to spread Your Graces, scales correlative with the agencies of Light matter cannot be used to size these habitual earthly curiosities for the reason that these devices do not reduce to these realms. Positively, you can conceptualize the experience and count the height of the hill or the quantity of what was secured, but there can be no uniqueness certified from these accomplishments that stretches its force to spaces outside the physical. While not to be condemned in and of themselves, the physical scores are largely not of the nature of Self-completions that lengthen outside of the habitations of Earth. Likewise, without a graceful intent when pursuing these interests, there is no memory from their completion more remote than what you can see, feel, and hear with the senses, or from what 3D scientific disciplines accept.

Counter to the earthly enticements, the repercussions from your Star source when you activate it by initiating an intention that has an affinity with the All, like tenderness, tolerance, goodness, gratitude, forgiveness, wishes for happiness and its causes to your brothers and sisters, patronage to Our best presence, and spreading You and your service for the point of enriching a manifestation of You, is transmitted to its correlating frequency outside the physical form upon launching the cognition. An emptiness of any sort is not to be known. This birthing transmission is sufficiently organic to tally on universal scales of equivalent nature that exist in the dominion where the force is gathered. There, purely 3D appropriations have no weight or sway.

Similarly, the human discoveries, while including techniques for calculating the money acquired or the number of passions fulfilled, do not encompass estimating techniques for quantifying productions with which it is not fully in sync, such as those breedings disseminated from a province outside the workings of the human eye.

You never were convinced that the Earth mindset as to what is viable to measure was the exclusive science for quantifying all phenomena positioned in the untold continuums. There is a conspicuous question mark when you have taken in even a glimpse of the mastery of the Graces, thrusting You out of the physical boundaries of earth, air, fire and water. What is the quality of that which gets thrust from within, and into what? As sure as it is an energetic thought structure, it is propelled. Just as certain is that there is a type of scale outside of Earth's sphere that gauges the hierarchy of the propulsion you administer.

Drawing a distinction between the characteristics of your material production vs. Your Ethereal production is a training that guarantees you the knowledge of those activities bringing maximal return during Your in-between state here on Terra.

Examining not an object or physical outcome, but an idea, and without a scale?

Thoughts are passed through invisible signals emitted from the material satellites. The Earth scientists detect this signal, but not with their eyes. And a graceful thought or action cannot emit from you a quantifiable healing resonance to sectors of existence unknown to your eyes?

That there is, the scale of your Light intellect computing from angles outside of present-day imaginative constructs. It exists in those sectors where you make multiple appearances simultaneously outside of your physicality. Debuts of You occur in the space you consider universes. These same universes you sometimes believe are exactly next to you, but it is only with your narrow view that you can't access them.

23: DIVINING TOOLS FOR YOU

The program feasible for you, in which you may judge the depths, breadths, degrees, magnitudes, and frequencies of your ingenuity in either: inventing this ever-morphing intelligent awareness with acts of loving kindness toward Yourself and others; or in collecting the whimsical strands, is justifiably confined to what you classify as Self-introspection. The explanation for the availability of only this type of inspection process coincides with the most crucial reason of your Being on Terra. That is, for now, the Cosmic system set where there are no automated mechanisms external to you for you to employ for comparing the worthiness of the properties of purely earthly pursuits vs. earthly bound Ethereal undertakings is because the plan for you being here in 3D is to originate the rubric that will inform you of the precise willfully designed actions you can take that will perpetuate the Self's majesty in prospering while surrounded by the dense swirlings of Earth. Alternatively phrased, it is the manner employed by your unconditional Core substance to understand the magnification of its resonance to points beyond where it currently resides by way of using its expertise to manifest Self-love while encased partially within what is experienced as taut matter. Some call it energetic evolvement. Thus, what awaits is your interactive, comparative analysis through earthly eyes, not the perception of a machine from another time and place.

Toiling on Terra?

For now, the level of Earth's frequency configurations permit only this mode of operation in order to calculate where upon the frequency ladder your maneuvers stand. But, lest you not forget since all is progress, that on another fine day, the "higher minds" of certain ilks within Earth's scientific community, or otherwise, who are encoded with the tools to manipulate energy with less need for Self-industry than you presently perceive it will reveal unique stylizations of matter. These creations you will recognize as devices that will lessen the effort you need so as to flow more freely into your desired destination; whether it be a purer reverberation or an alternative spatial positioning.

That fine day has not arrived. So, in the Now, don't underestimate the wondrousness of your industry. You are the identity of the Who that actuates the All to this position that is to be reached on "another fine day." Thus, the seemingly greater ease will have been a result of, yes, your toil.

This avoids the more important point.

Conceded. This purpose is subordinate to the explanation known in certain areas of the Expanses where they value you administering your mastery so as to transfigure those preoccupations that keep you in cozy bondage. They have their own vantage point for prizing this application of your work.

Your imagination is fertile. Undeniably, even this utility is not the final edge to the gem. Let's start this way: if you could take from a machine you don't understand markings that inform of the constricting options available within the cozy slumbers, and also, if the instrument would display the worth and nature of the exact disciplines that will bring you Lighter-weight expansions, your choice of the roads to travel would likely be greatly influenced by this otherworldly automation. You will agree to the automation's judgment as a conceptual fact. You then conduct your life according to this machine and thus avoid intermingling with most of Life's energies.

There are a few drawbacks to this: reading a computation of this sort would have little importance to you because it could never reveal to your earthly brain, currently challenged somewhat by earthly senses, the properties of the substance it measures. More important, the machine would hold for you the most vital flaw/ contradiction to the cause of your existence on Earth: detainment from your energetic maturation. These somewhat ineffectual conclusions you will rely upon. There will be no effort you will commit to locating your individual interpretation of why you remain spellbound within stale tales of meager glories. Without exertion you will put on hold the understandings you are ordained to acquire as to how to dissolve what according to universal laws will be the repeated rounds of "confusion" hitting you with a different cover until you solve their riddle. There you will sit, alone and feeling small, with baffling mysteries gnawing the life from you. The stupors in emotional upheavals will remain.

Actualization of the biggest Self from the most diverse angles!

Most definitely. The machine is incapable of interpreting to you your Self-worth. This translation you are to make is the only path out of unsettling meagerness. The machine's supposition just won't do.

Coddling this guesswork, you then make no effort to Self-disclose the explanations as to the truth of You. This is the only Self-disclosure of any relevance to achieving and sustaining a non-fluctuating reverberation a notch above your current status. It is this quest you miss where you have not only a special right, but obligation, according to the universe's natural forces, to cognize and display attributes synonymous with knowing You or your affinities with the Graces. Your natural likeness to the Graces are the trustworthy and legitimate You. The process of removing the haze and seeing this authenticity of You is singularly instituted with the combination of behavior and thought only you decide will deliver it when you make choices during episodes where fierce assaults entreat you to submit to thrills unworthy of You. You have the opportunity to decide upon the thrills worthy of You. The uniqueness of this blend in Your earthly setting is never-ending.

Now, back to the point of the decisive reason that your Self-ingenuity and not a machine is used on Earth for guiding you into a familiarity with undertakings that permit sustained prosperity. Without having lived this process that activates the knowledge of your Self's nobility, you could not originate these inimitable manifestations that compliment your Original Source. This is the stock We covet.

US and others?

US is the evolution of Us and other sentient beings. The nucleus of the matter you mobilize when putting into play this merging with Me in order to pronounce the "Self" is the structuring of creations for which humanity has not shaped a communication that effectively describes it. Your discovery of this combination establishes You into a more diverse All. Therefore, and again, obeying machines just will not do. And here you have your answer. This "curiosity" in Self-love you propagate is not merely a nutrient for you, but one coveted by the multifaceted components of combined existences, propagations that occur only with the rarity of your devise. It is an elevation of the Self of most pristine sort, oftentimes labeled as "ascension" for the All.

Those who have not taken on so many pretender visions digest the presence of the Graceful virtues in Self-Love as they reverberate through the tides of their demonstration. It is there that they break down the whimsical apparitions when these currents draw near to their emotional bodies. For these individuals, reliable demarcations to the motives or thought forms which merit the Self have been made. Although, even for these individuals, on each presentation of a defeating energy, they put to the test their place in the Ethereal Mountains as they apprehend the dense quality of that which diverges from Them. Appreciating the debilitations of the densities, these souls have mostly extricated themselves from the need for the severity of the testing you have brought upon yourself.

For you, it is necessarily more complex. You have a thirst to possess a mental schematic that you believe educates your mind and "Soul" on the reason for granting purpose to lift yourself out of energies disfiguring accurate viewpoints of You. The hardened practical route, that is. Know that this manner of measuring is of your narrow construct, unsanctioned by any authority but you. Albeit, it allows you peace in your decision and oftentimes much distress during the regimen.

Of course, it is no surprise to you that even this exercise of yours, when concluded for the end of growing in Self-love, is a priceless construct of the Graces.

24: THE INDUCTION'S IMPETUS

Your inquisitiveness becomes your induction into what you see as more credible systems for weighing the universal imprint of your pursuits here on Terra. Most impressively, the I in the sky sees your commitment to search for the identity of the confinements within the old doctrines you have built, as shown by your gallant attentiveness and open heart inclined to supplant all archaic modes. This is the creed to seating each of your endeavors on the rung to Your rising which is justifiable on scales of universal altitude.

You once over vacillate with nearly debilitating doubt arising from your desire to give protection to that special whimsical of your adoration.

Has your thinking brain ever given the word *sincere* its proper meaning when it comes to accepting where you frequently place your daily enthusiasms? You source for a gold outside of these earthly callings, and still, your exertions in vocations beneficial to broadening returns for You are patently subordinate to those handed over to collecting the whimsical strands.

You plod on, scaling numerous terrestrial cliffs in the hunt for a cure to the internal turmoil you have been battling to work out for your entire life. These stirrings in the physical have not allayed the angst, regret, and ravenous appetite that cannot be quenched.

No, you cannot claim a surety that you walk through your finite days on this go-around on Terra while having sighted the ambit of the adaptations of sustainable joy available to you by way of the smart words of another. Wholly from your radical comparison process is where you will uncover unforgettable indicators announcing to You which of your affairs is taller and finer and which continues outside the flesh, or is a production of your physical victory. Your foreign ruler will be seen.

There are leaps of faith you must try on for a while to go forward with this operation in estimation of the Ethereal Graces within the limits of 3D words and techniques. And hopefully, this is one that is sound in logic. You hold at least one present-day saturation operating in a mode that depletes your daily endurance and refracts the Light of your Star away from its equals. This depleter is adequate to employ as a sample in Our comparative diagnosis. Your cherished warm and fuzzy will establish for you that it is an anomaly to the Star's constitution once you behold its restraining traits.

The I in the sky wanders from the point, being that your consciousness is limber with the hope of transforming with Self-love the total variety of grim rulings inundating you. These other single-dimension ravages at times unsteady you. It is a fact that WE have pledged to a plan for extracting their sanctums linked to your frames. The I in the sky confirms that these lies you repeat to yourself will become extraordinarily obvious as nothing more than confusions:

- You are alone in solitude
- Your difficulties have taken your freedom
- Your resentments paralyze you
- You have no energy to guide those in your charge
- No incentive brings life into your veins
- You can't reposition from being seized by another's will
- Standing alone and strong will leave you lonely
- Not seeing a clear path in your mind inhibits your progress
- The soothing and nearsighted goal you desire is preferable to inquiring within to source the key to a bright future
- It is not possible to untie the strings encircling you in a meaningless life
- Standing with love in your heart when you give to help another has no value unless tangible results are achieved
- You can't apologize because it will invite vulnerability

- Forgiving will leave you impotent
- There is no strength in kindness
- You do not have enough resourcefulness to thrive in your career
- Money is the only abundance that is faithful
- Sadness consumes you
- You suffer a shortage of excitement for anything but the basic desires, and these are the excesses that focus your day—the desire, alcohol, substances, and food—all of which are sufficient for now.

Your speculation is confirmed. The above states of inertness are predicted to systematically fall by the wayside upon the rush of Light matter to be released when you eradicate the "one" laying siege to crucial aspects of your power Center, to which We return.

As it is currently postured, this exceptional attack you continually undergo is caustic enough in warm and fuzzy contentment that it counters any unbiased and critical analysis of it. And so, until it is adequately distanced from your bodies to permit your unbiased insight into its makeup, We may not employ it as a comparator to Your natural likeness with the Graces. Earth scientists call it an addiction, an acquiescence to the seductions of a critically dense substance that is whirling the Earth that has attached to you, sullying your Star. Give it a name. For some of your Earth brothers and sisters, it is the school of highest education and the most precarious tightrope. It is not always relative to a substance or person. Idea constructs guiding you into oblivion are equally as caustic, and often are associated with a physical obsession. Imagine the density brought upon your Star's Light when you commit to condemning, to revenge, to being "right", to "justice", to being the "victim", or when you align with the need to control the definition of what is "decent".

Fortunately, however, it is this uniquely superlative and seductive tendency of yours that can show the clearest contrast for your inspection when comparing the whimsicals and the Graces once you attain the frame of consciousness to bring nonpartisan scrutiny to it. Ergo, to know the base existence of its sensory pitch, you must step back from its dominance.

This is the diluted version the I in the sky brings me? Have you not missed a relevant step? You mean to inform me that this initiatory exercise in fasting from the fixation will give me the eyes of knowledge as I touch its primitive seeding while ripping it from my bodies?

It is you who created the need for Me to impart the information with less than direct particulars.

But, yes, the brave solution to reaching a reliable conclusion as to the hierarchy of this warm and fuzzy is to dissect it as you "rip" it, or should you choose, "tactfully declaw" it, together with your bands of brothers and sisters in the Light. There, you have the more vivid picture you have requested.

Certainly, also, you will witness it with greater objectivity subsequent to the declawing, having let go of your own preoccupation with it.

There can be no accurate vision of the depleter while you are conjoined. Care to take a look?

You resist, assuming your currently perceived objectivity toward this tactile fixation is fine to use for mastering a vision of Your extended outposts next to this depleter of Us.

The I in the sky proposes that homage to your adventure can be simplified by your agreeing that there is no sacrifice too large, including forgoing sensory "reliefs" in 3D, if in renouncing you free thoroughfares leading to messages that tell your dreary slumbers in pain, despair, angst, hunger, or thirst. These are the states that erode Your attentiveness to My voice, which, when known, you will want for nothing. You having a sureness that you will envisage these revelations is the means to instigating you to bust the stranglehold you may not have noticed as your playmates, covering the beams detaining you in outdated "truths."

Subtle changes in your bodies that make 3D functioning more impressive you have previously noted. After this course, the "tuning up" of your operable Earth vessel will be unmistakable. You will be at the onset of touching the future you seek of generating from Your heightened ingenuity, all it is You so will.

25: LOCATING THE CREED

What the I in the sky classifies as an unrelenting domination of my most inner structures of energy due to my preoccupation with it is also the only amusement I recognize.

The topic you cite, your melodramatic bathing within another's sentiments of a proposed love for you while pretending it is the epitome of every beauty and tenderness, you have already succinctly admitted as a mistake; that this bath was, in fact, your quest for Yourself, which is not to be known from these sentiments. Since you have finally conceded your pretext in this amusement, there is no haze upon your Star to diffuse.

The insipid vapor deadening your senses and directing you into further oblivion is the very addiction you refute as an enslavement.

It comes to pass—your primal scream organized by Me due to your fixation's stranglehold. Its identity you admit. Your wailing for the opportunity to be that agile being you recall when separating from the Light of Creation has been used to further introduce you to Me. And from there, the tumbling of your misconception that carrying on with this obsession of yours will allow you to satisfy your undertaking to be informed as to whether or not you are truly barred from accessing other rooms that wait for your elucidation. To receive the information instructing you to the way of your release from bondage the arteries of communication between Us need freed. To the unwary, take care: relinquishing Your dominator for the decisive amount of time to answer your query may spark the flawed suspicion that you do not understand even your name and its purpose. Be glad, for you are not of faint of heart when completing Our ambitions. All those treks in physical mastery pale in comparison. Nonetheless, in due course, there will be a reinvigoration caught by your eyes while you are at the top of your mountain. There you are to learn the depleter is no longer the guardian to your cave.

You swiftly surmounted this brand-new state of mind. The pleasure of an innocent child is your transitional response to My proposal of this scholarly discipline in analytical relativity as to the materials that weight and that lighten your life. The peril of missed time with the whimsicals does not chafe when you reflect upon the importance of what you leave behind in relation to the advent of your association with numerous gateways into uttermost peripheral vision. With admiration I studied how you arrived at this bracing for your uprising against the dominance of the leeches. The other physical dangers you have faced in life which actually subjected you to physical harm is unlike this proposition. Your sole deficit in this quest may be one of a social nature, of being re-classified as less than what modern society considers a successfully "engaging" human being.

Your ever-true Earth partner, the "persuader" for you to accept this bid, is this: in this life of finite chances You agreed to test the mettle of every plank you believe you have caught sight of that seems to impose an upper limit. Your speculations upon the diversity of the planks are vast.

This persuader is an invitation without a loss.

Yes, the trial at hand, telling the actual step you make in eclipsing your preceding circumstances, will end with no dissipation. The conclusion will be a more open ended transference of information between Us.

26: THE DARE TO INITIATION ACCEPTED

The rush of tingling throughout your skin is Me, shedding Etheric tears of joy. It is My characteristic reply when the I in the sky is cloaked at the onset of your birth in Self-love by way of your plunge into researching undiscovered aspects of Your Star. You draw from seas beyond Me. An intractable color ray in a piece of an ascending platform is placed with your launching into the Beauties you have every intention to maintain. No want will ever be noted from this inauguration, unlike the spirit of victory being vanquished after the race you won or the scholarly problem you solved as displays of your practice in functional mastery.

27: THE REPELLER OF THE HARD SHOT FROM THE WHIMSICALS

Awarding consequence to your life based upon societal opinions, whether from the majority or its subcomponents, is a shot from the whimsicals. Being shaken at this stage of disengaging from your subduer is a shove to the surface of certain collateral reasoning you have also consented to straightening. Dislodging ideas you consider components to your security and which never were is a multi-layered process that involves differentiating between the earthly energies consuming you and You as a multidimensional existence. Part of this operation involves quelling societal conditioning that you often use as a basis for approval, as opposed to your Star's instructions. These hits luring you to agree to cultural norms as your guideposts in plotting your tracks permeate further after you recently gave the edicts of society the authority to rule you. This conjecture that any other's customs are useful to You is futile; you have yielded to the beacon of your Star.

The bids from the whimsicals to join them, if proven to convince you, will spread the ambit of your earthly time as it is on this day dispensed, stagnant. And staying static, as is, you chance a future regret that—with no time to rearrange it in five, ten, twenty, or even worse, in thirty years, when you come to the persuasion that you wish to present your utmost to those of your warm devotion, all there will be to share is an inert experience of the mundane. You will be left with an inept presence. Due to previous apportionments you may have divvied up over time to components encompassed solely in the physical and other confusions, in the future there can be no airlifting you to Our apex so that you may impart rarefied points of view that are heartening to you and those you choose to endow with your accumulations in a bit of universal genius.

Airlifting scatters the pieces in places too far and wide for you to assemble any outline adequate for helpful perceptions. You will become dizzy from the heights and be incapable of absorbing your insights with any clarity. In these future times, lowly attachments, something like a choking on earthly energies, will still be hampering your strength and literally choking your energetic bodies. Be assured that you will not live the Graces' wise glow that you are more than curious about while you maintain your preoccupations with the status quo.

This perseverant throbbing is not overcome.

Did you not say many times in solemn truth that it was your dream to behold You, the You that you now vaguely envision as the author of your Star, with keener eyes, and to speak with greater command of who You are and from what you are conceived? Assuredly you did at a time when the line of communication between Us was without uprisings. Accordingly, the steady thumping. Delay is no longer a potential to dream of. This drive carries You and Me and every adventurer; unknown, it strides with Us side by side.

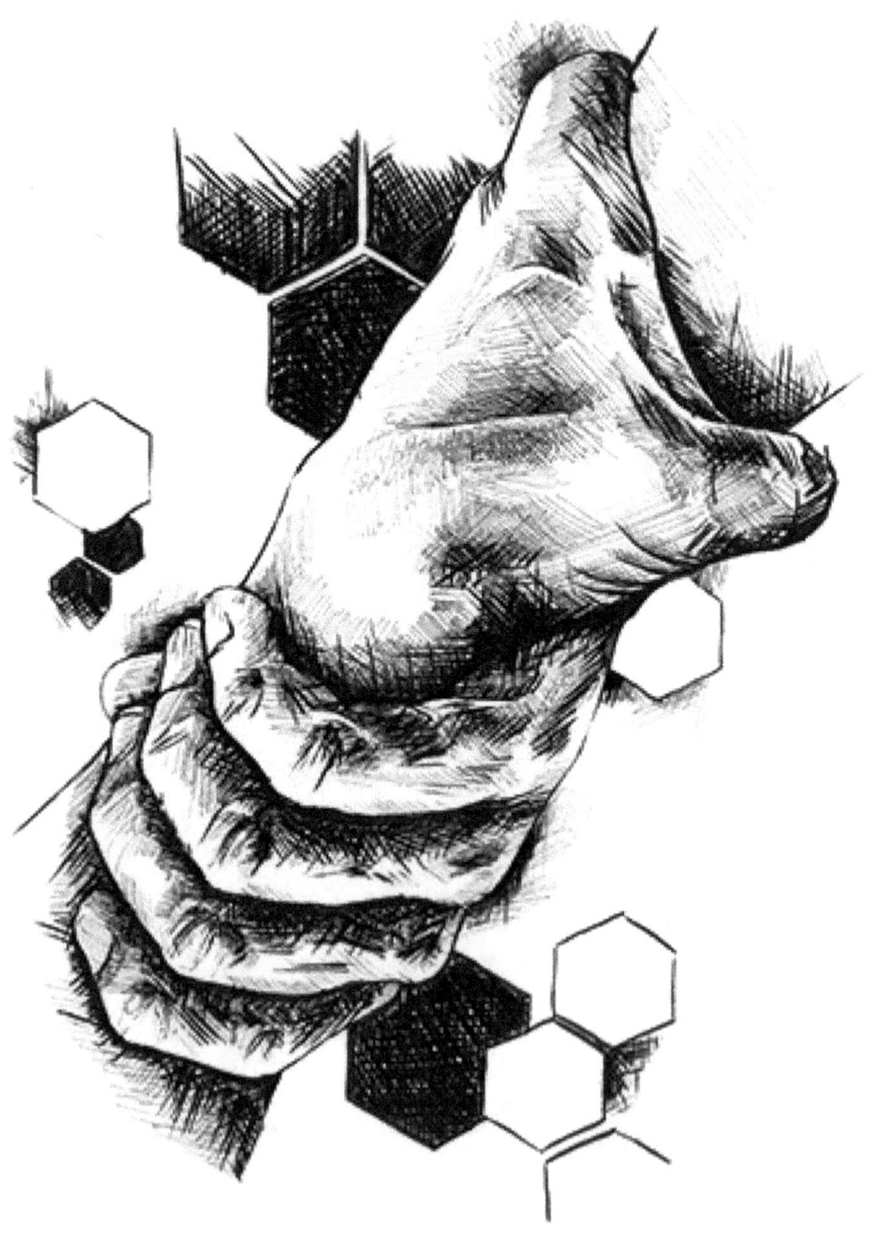

28: COMMANDING THE INITIATION

You rise to defy.

When one watches a hellacious battle being fought for freedom of the one wrongfully imprisoned, words don't suit to communicate the sight. Tears are the outcome when that Me here, who in your mind still floats on clouds, is a guest at your side of this beginning you have enlisted in. The I in the sky samples a bit of the excellence You projected into your consciousness. It is a fact that no stumbles are elegant. The screams in anger during points of desperation from being battered with the abrupt infiltrations, that there proved no point in resisting the irresistible and insatiable warm and fuzzy constrictions to your vitality, gave way for a respite and a regrouping. The speculation of "just once more" were the attacks of the squelching creatures. To look upon their antagonistic claws, as I do in the Ethereal, would be to enjoy the superior position you shaped to show your care for You. With the wailings to the heavens for allowing this, there sprang the life you gave to an instinct, that you will survive to look upon the resolutions to the mysteries confining you, and that it was You and Me for special reasons, and not the heavens, that brought you here.

You met with finesse the shadowy crew squatting in your world, taking note of the crudeness of their chokehold, even gleaning the appearance of your hand in combining with the hand choking you. Then, the supremely cruel apparition: that there was nothing else to you other than this whimsical concoction and that you had no other relevance and no other form prevailing outside of your earthly vessel, a most oppressing image. You overpowered this delusion by seeing beyond that strangling hand to the object of Our Heart's choice, and there you were totally absorbed in the Love of You. The hand you observed as your own was now touching a hand of Light emanating from the Heart of the All and the Heart of you.

Did it take two spans of years or did it take ten? The spans are only seen as convergences around the etchings of Self-love.

The me that is here measures five spans of years!

From the silhouette of the cruelties I saw you up against, this small length of time comments on your willingness. It is not until this will is shown that you touch the Hand you remember reclaiming You.

Commanding your world will be Our finale and your future. This fractional recovery of You dismantled any expectations you may have had that a bright, shiny goal in matter awaits. You desire the expertise to govern your world so that there will be little effect upon it by the bullies, as opposed to a shiny prize. You have achieved the feat of entering the center of your Star's steady clam even when surrounded by these torrents of density.

WE rose in unison as a last act to watch the particles obliterated from your bodies, an additional introduction to Your Star having been made.

Shedding shackles is not for the lighthearted. It overturns many explanations I had of me.

This resolute joy of Self you brought to bear morphed the shadow substance into the stock of Self-worth. That beguiling tingle buzzing your head came from the far-reaching cheers of your brothers and sisters. Thank them for their mantra. You may not have adequately heard: "Your life has great meaning and you are loved."

29: ALLIES IN BALANCE

Now evacuated from the anesthetics of the once cozy slumber, you arrive at the line of your zeal, the demarcations you sowed from the ferocious choice to love You. To you, the line represents what you crossed when you withdrew from being in bondage to fleeting satisfactions. There is where you left it, for good reason, after you had lived out the disproportionate fondness you had for these depleters. At this stage, you commemorate the line as a wall that you inserted for your refuge from enslavement. Although, one day, this wall is to be seen an equalizer of a segment of the universal You, which hangs in the balance of many spaces. This time will come. You quiver at even approaching the subject of why the wall exists. Know that you will arrive at an image of the embankment as a symmetry of dependable, streaming Light. There are no variables to this exact closure.

Forward to your future: Your formerly entwined preoccupation that you severed from your Star is classified as an incidental meddling that you only faintly recall as a savagery appended to the fringes of all of your bodies of energy.

30: THE CALCULATION

Your mention of the old playmate as an intruder reveals its endowments as dissimilar from the risings of your Star. In your venture for deciding where on the rung of phenomenon your earthly experience of the whimsical pleasures belongs, the I in the sky assists you. We figure out the peculiarity of their base voice by juxtaposing the features of what you witnessed being cleaved from your Ethereal and carnal being with that which can alter their constituents. The Affinities with You, or that which remolds the structure of the whimsicals, are gleamed into being when you intuit:

- Why you have chosen to leave behind the lies you have been telling about yourself so that you may face what needs correcting
- The pleasure of knowing you do not need to gossip or compare yourself to others to have an idea of your heavenly coordinates
- Liberation from the fears of jealousy by being secure in the fact that what our brother possesses of enduring worth, you also carry
- Discovering what it is to offer from your heart to a loved one your finest qualities while accepting that the only important gratitude is for having the opportunity to do so
- That it feels hollow to take more than you have earned
- That nothing is truly lost and only gain is attained by addressing your motives without coloring their tone

- That holding hope dear in the face of panic is a discovery beyond compare
- That taking more than you give creates imbalance
- That speaking untruthfully skews everyone's playing field and sets the stage for a coming implosion into darkness as the opening to the last act of a deceptive play
- The unmistakable, damning nature to you and the other when you utter an opinion that you do not believe
- That no longer wanting to blame another allows the door to the offering of forgiveness
- That there is no space in a tranquil heart for the idea of pride or embarrassment, for the Star can have no pride or disgrace
- The enjoyment taken from a state of humbleness or humility when you acquire a practical and transient "victory"
- The elation from not causing jeopardy to another when the opportunity for vengeance knocks
- Offering a restored heart, free from bitterness, to your brother after you separated from the hurt you held from being hit with his avenging behavior
- Training the mind to project hope into another's forlorn heart, all the while you profoundly trust that a thought of this magnitude has been received by the one in need
- That it is a chain of ruinous association to agree that you need to punish another for an offense inflicted upon you
- Excessive indulgences feed only earthly whimsicals
- That the freedoms you have had before you, even if just to breathe and show love while in your highly tuned and empathetic vessel, are treasures
- That control and conquest in the material have an empty cadence when exercised for reason of power over others
- That it is not denouncement and judgment of your brother that heals this other, it is compassionate acceptance that he is in his pain
- That available and within your province are the resources of a never ending or beginning eternity.

Tally the character of some of these Affinities with You that have no qualities that interface with physically perceptible acquisitions or sensual encounters. I propose that, as part of the diagnosis, you appraise what is required to initiate the rush of the Affinities' placid confidence when you are faced with chaos, which lasts as long as you give them deserving attention. Agreed, no physical stimuli is necessary for them to serve you. Verify as well that they hold a composure and luminosity that satiates the heart. The aptitude of these ideations to prolong Self-fulfillment with merely your imaginative flair establishes that their attributes can be upheld without external support. Next, rate the wholeness derived from your generating these Affinities. No input, let alone sensory, can make these jolts more rewarding. A pining for greater achievement is not an attribute from their experience. Confluences in these states of wholeness have no want for more. And fear, sadness, pain, and guilt do not accompany them, nor can these states of illusion lessen the coalition you make with them.

The omniscience within the Graces disables the impairing myths that induce confusion and paralysis into humanity.

Then, finally, ask whether you perceive a final point as to their ends? No, for they are a case of supremacy sweeping into extensions circumscribed only by the magnanimous intentions you may shine forth through your Star center. What is more, the Star Core has no borders. When you embody the Light, mental dance of these Affinities, you twirl in a world that resounds in destinies with intelligences not entirely triggered by you, to date. You can revive them to be as pronounced as the time you constituted them.

Distinct from Our Affinities are the whimsicals. Their features are impermanent in the wake of their merriments. Just as the winds rid the snow of prints, the casual amusements fade from the lofty spot on which you tried to pin them. In fact, bring back from your past when you strove to make the whimsical grander by overdosing your enterprising will with satisfactions for the body, for material security, or even for power over others. You agonized to position these diverting entertainments within this spot of the Infinite Solids. The topmost mark of your contentment in their area of amusement was met, although you refused to accept it, preferring to force the square of the whimsical into the Star of the Affinities. It is here that you came to know insatiability. There was a finite nature to the effects to be realized. The pulsing indulgence kept you searching for a higher turf in its playground, where there was none. As you closed your eyes, the deceit pretended for you that it could hoist you to where the issuances of the Affinities you have with the Graces sit with You. When you united with them to accept this unattainable ambition, well, you lived the explosions hitting Us. The substances, objects, places, and faces where you implanted your lofty ideals left complexities in ill-apportionment. We now disentangle. A prolonged satisfaction from acquisitions, control, sensuality or extravagance in consuming food or substances was not to be realized no matter how ingenious the machinations were to squeeze these friendly tendencies into the spacious Light. On every occasion the I in the sky surveyed it was your combining with compatriots in pain, regret, despair and fear.

Chasing after a trustworthy gratification using components that cannot construct it mingles you into disorientation, thus enchanting the clamoring disturbances.

Inertias don't unite with Light, but are converted by it.

Discordant brutalities. They were pieces of my bodies!

Your mental, physical, and emotional bodies.

31: OUR INNOVATIONS

Situations normally laced with sadness, despair, or regret you no more live as messages in dread. You see them as barely even pelts of gray matter, sliding by the outer edge of your concentration. Never before have you seen the subtle sharpness to colors, which is now your pleasant fascination. Sounds even transfer with them novel accents that speak the prose of your heart. Your body, filled with greater mechanical verve, can accomplish more mental and physical tasks with less effort. And fragrances are recalled, their scents magnified. Your energy has had a rare upgrade. Your Star is devoid of many tiresome encumbrances.

32: NEW CORRIDORS

Corridors have been enlivened by way of this valuation exercise. Your earthly vessel has better receptiveness for Light immersion so that you may compose with levity when you come upon your many future training episodes. The new pathways are there for you to pass onto those you aspire to inspire. The amelioration of astral brutalities likewise ignited an increased rate in the burning of dust from your prized Illuminator. A by-product is depth perception into what betrays You and what joy is prepared with and for You. Illustrative suggestions directing you to where We can have more favorable ends are no more a blur of meaningless scenery. A rejection, an acceptance, a glance or quick word from a stranger, even failures to notice or sudden curiosity about what otherwise is a "common" condition to you. You are having the "Self" control to allow the timing of events to sync, noticing that they fit like a curious new beginning. The Star's ready and willing voice is unmistakable. Haphazard, like your old habits, it is not.

You gently admit that the network you blamed Me for throwing you into is not the warm and fuzzy fellowship you for so long soothed yourself into accepting, only to notice the tight grip that prohibited ties to Our heightened acquaintances. MINE is replete with you executing plans within mansions that contain passages shepherding you into a myriad of lanes, all of which magnify the abilities of yours, which please Us. The Star's blaze torched the bramble, imparting onto you these endless channels where you will operate in states of tact qualified to bring about the mission of your Star.

The choice is a diamond's edge in your mind: move with miscalculations into adversity or enroll in Curriculums that will break through your heavily guarded misperception that mastery of your world is not within your realm of competence?

PART V: EXPANDING THE LABELS

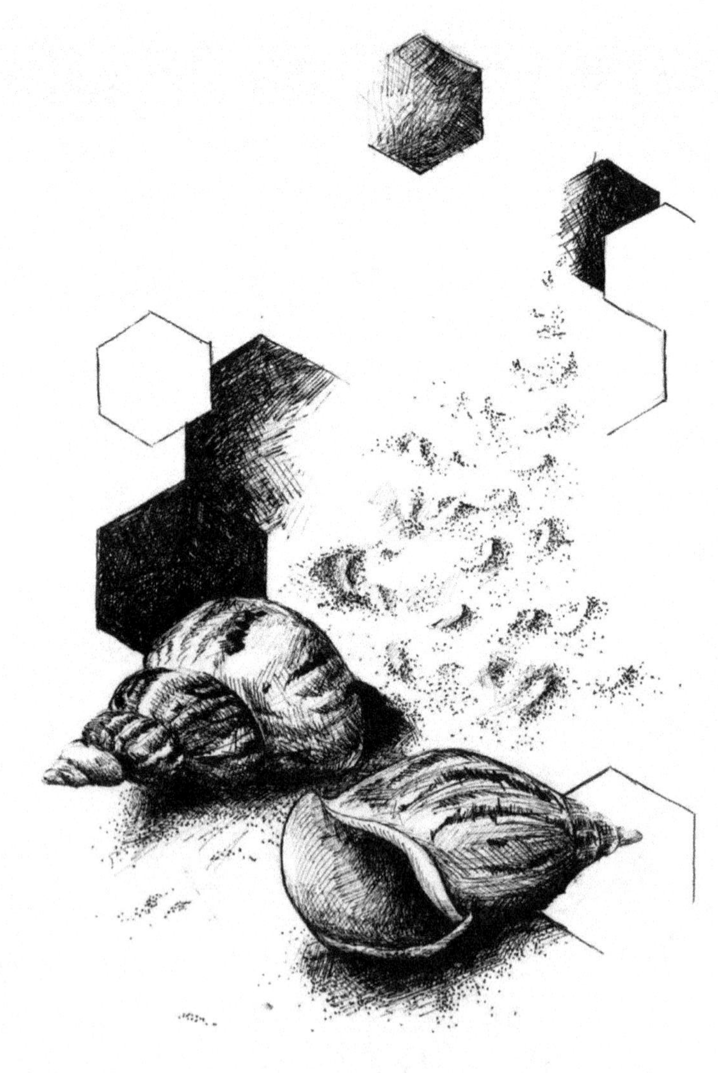

33: ENRICHING THROUGH SENTIMENTS OF "LOSS"

You become the pressure you create with your agonizing that "loss" and "failures" are and were of your experience.

Your ripening Lighter frames decrease the stresses of anger you have for the myth of your "loss." But, it does not filter into all.

The earmark of *failures* has preoccupied you at numerous exits out of past dustings. The conventional emotion of *loss* or *failure* having its onset with a disappearance of any sort from your life is a push for you to convert it into an alternative nuance. Ordinary connotations when using the terms *loss* and *failure* you have never been at home with. Designating as a personal diminishment the removals of your personal fellowships forgets the evolutionary aspect of what the I in the sky calls "initiatory arrangement in fresh conditions." The likenesses you have to all that hovers above the weighty pulls prescribe that you leave to the margins of your life ineffective engagements with "loss." Changes by way of absences in materiality or personages have made room for the excursions that embolden what We pursue. Characterizing defeat or loss as modern norms do eliminates the wisdom earned. You knew no loss or failure, only a parting of ways with sentimental irrelevance and density.

An uncomfortable proposition when you feel sentimental tears from within.

Sadness: the thought calamity of not liking the true state of facts.

Take away from these words the lifelong messages in defeat you have ascribed to them. Ruthless energies you sense as dire emotions have you believing that you have lost or failed. They impair management of a life in gratification. Saturation in "loss" and its attendant state of "sadness" activates the birth of a body for these terms, and with it your Core is listless.

The full appearance of the intricacies oppressing your Star are unknown to you. However, you have committed to Me that the sole loss to which you will accredit any validity is a temporary loss of sheen from your Star, that is:

- When you brush off honesty
- When you use an ignorant excuse to push accuracy's glare into the shadows
- When you give less value to kindness, generosity, or forgiveness and extol insolence
- When control is what you compare to being whole
- When you blame others for your predicament, which incapacitates your attempts toward mastery
- When you fail to carry love and strength in your heart, thoughts, actions, and words
- When you condemn what you don't fully understand
- When you do not cherish every breath in this Earth vessel
- When you lessen your outlook by narrowing your choices by seeing only the option of expressing anger, damaging you and the other.

And yes—believing that your champion Illuminator can exist in the same space as lazy comforts and excessive Earth elations that overdose the Lighter and physical frames into complacency. Disregarding these standards, there is a dwindling of the infusion of momentum into Our Star's Command Center, but no loss to the You we research; only a distraction from Our communion.

Refresher: Not too far from this day, you shaped a shining sculpture out of "losing" a material possession and an earning. The brightness came from its embodiment etched out of honesty, and understanding as to why you respected truth in the face of overwhelming duress to acquire for the ego and to accommodate physical tastes in excess. Also, you "lost" a squatter within your autonomous Star Center when you took back your free will from another. WE don't need to reference the recent severing of that mass, nauseating you with intense lethargy. Your Star's valuation preceptor was the tool to "lose" the whimsicals, or to eliminate the cracks for the whimsicals to enter and satiate you. All were "finds" from "losses." Any name will do.

This meaning given to the word "loss" expels all hold on you of lack, as well as the smudge upon your Star.

You worry about emptiness. Companionship with your Star's relational standards is Our ultimate fellowship.

Reassemble troublesome compositions of thought: Never let it escape you that you cheat all fallow sentiment of a life with your choosing not to give it your life's moments. By bestowing any connotation of defeat upon Our helpful disengagements—giving a spirit to the words *sadness* and *loss*—you stifle your delivery into the *more* that you now relate to as the recognition of *more* of You.

Your mood is infused with improved knowledge of Our Affinities—and We are perched, observing from the pinnacle, a flushing in being You.

34: MOURNING THE WARM AND FUZZIES

Still, you have theories of "vacancies" due to absent playmates. These imposters are faintly clinging to your bodies. Temporarily, you re-enter the simile of you shrouded in the haze. As you have done, you may choose to fade into the dimness where the experience of Your full volume was being repressed. To mourn history gives your life to pointlessness; a swirling disorienting you into the conclusion that you are "defective" without the dear associate of your fondness.

Detail what it is *not*. When one who helped tie you to this Earth has cut the celestial cord secured to their physical build and has been re-acclimated into a body of a different span of space and a more agile weight—this is not the vacancy you speak of. While their higher tie to Earth is cut from the one of your tender devotion, there remains a solemn intimacy in your earthly reality that is truly unavailable, but not due to any clearing of your Star, as is the circumstance you now grieve. The ultimate "missing" from your life on Terra has an unavoidable course to run when those who have helped settle you to Terra leave her soil. It may be that your loved one who departed Terra's soil was the sole presence welding You to the Earth's variety of brilliances. Nevertheless, even after this changeover of your loved one (and later your absorption in emotional abandon, refusal to believe, heartache, and cursing your existence), you dug for relief from despair, and it was there.

On the cusp of your consciousness, you fancied a sensitivity that relays an enchanting meaning to you: that while her exact frame in 3D is no longer, she nowadays savors the broader exposition of being alive in her new inhabitance, or likely multi-inhabitances, and more so than she did on Earth's surface. Even the enfolding of yourself in anger and self-pity was spirited away when you caught the flashback to what you have repeatedly held in your Heart, that life is eternal with wings to fly. Disbanding merciless imposters ushered you into the attraction of your loved one existing as a bird who has just recovered her wings, no more exposed to the weight of the Earth plane. You saw her voyage being consumed in love and flashes of eternity that lured your precious one. Wiped out was the big deception you agonized in, the unkind instruction laid down upon you and all there on Terra by the raging illusionists, that this primordial structure of you on Earth is the only region in which You are capable of making an appearance. You were even pervaded by the sight of transmigrations of You moving upwards to the Central Sun, changing hue, structure, and thickness, thus alleviating your notion of what is the truest sense on Earth, a 3D "loss." You then took in an amazing treat, seeing the unbroken perpetuation of Our nature. The melancholy and longing softened.

Agony in lowly regrets stemming from a displaced partner is a choice, just as was your separating their intolerable appendage from You. This is not to say that you are not sensing a syndrome, which is notable. The one-time partner corded to your lighter weight bodies by the intensity of the adoration you surmised they should have. There are those who call it nostalgia, remembrances of threads of consummate contentment in routine fun, which enlivens a reluctance to avow the truth—that you are whole without external support. Thus, the mourning. You grieve for Your neglected Star-Self, but believe that you grieve for the other. Getting engrossed in views of yourself as a needy being that diminishes without another, which is a somewhat pitiful version of the entirety of You, keeps the nostalgia close, as does a comforting blanket for a child still wounded from leaving the luxury of the womb. It is a given that, as to the hours of complacent amusements with the partner, there is a partial deconstruction from their fibers interlaced with yours that occurs to sections of your energetic figuration. What you lugged around with you for so long will disencumber you in the span of time you wish, subject to your book of illustrations losing the one depiction, that the infatuations were more than passing amusements with a few educational embedments. Decide that from your earthly inhabitance you will effectuate the You that manages to overflow into the All with only the first-rate circuits compatible to fuel the Star's luminosity.

YOUR Fountainhead searches out the misleading pieces and puts them to rest by nudging your Heart-Mind to appraise and verify the actuality of your "mournful" experience approximate to Your sweeping durations into multitudes of octaves.

Eleven years is a fleeting delight?

For forty years fleeting. The union you mourn was not designed for Us to retain.

35: NEMESIS AS YOUR PROMOTER

"Nemesis," or Our provoking envoys, the whimsical subterfuges pressing Us not to reckon our Origin, are a cause for putting your leading qualities forth. While there is no basis in good sense to adopt them, they should eventually, when separated from their control of You to where you can call out their correct complexions, see them as building blocks. This will be the making of them and You into a Light carving.

Building blocks to hell.

It is hell because you chose not to pay any regard to Your majestic stature in the universe, again overcome by anger's tumult.

The intrigues of distortion, described as your enemy, share less of You when they face you in the rank of a particle accelerator for all you encounter. They are persuasive characters, illusionists, drawing arrangements of energy that pilot you into their sensibilities in all frivolities. Though never forget that they are the antidotes to any stagnation in You. They skillfully posture before you proposals. You then convert their suggestions into a renovation of You by shifting away from easy acquiescence to their open arms, while relinquishing any dread that they can be effectual in managing your life, and while burning in your mind the definite upper limits they can place on your freedom to fly. It is in this uncompromising stroke that you garner favorable assets, from you deciding how high you climb and not the whimsicals. This Heart-Mind activation is where you will no more behold the whimsicals as enemies, but as pastimes that once stopped you from tending to the picture show that was meant for only you to direct. Their Lighter configuration is a spinoff of your energetic alchemy.

PART VI: ACKNOWLEDGING OUR CHOICES

36: PREFERRING THE PARTNERS IN COMPETENCE

I speak to the I in the sky. It suits me fine to redesign the lines, refusing to enter into ill-conceived plays. These are exams from another day.

Your wanting words, agitated distractions. In this undercurrent that Me here is picking up on, your beast of no "opportune future" crushes you. Changing anxious disquiet into Light is the opportunity for you with a well partnered Us. The predicament, the Me that defines the other part of Us is oftentimes so sparsely affiliated with you that Our interchange is barely plausible to your thoughts. The mistake is your belief that the ravagers of your Star field make the decision to append you to their weights. This is an annihilating split between Us that can finish what you have only begun.

Electing to be tied to lost hope? It is not me who takes that choice.

It is a confounding notion, that you would decide on this life-negating disease. Though you do, as the very scourge you have chosen disguises with its staggering force the moment you make the actual decision to prefer disavowing Your reality. That matter hitting you with "no opportune future" is an especially strong strain, but still a ruse obscuring that it is your action to decide upon a union with victimhood and disempowerment. It is of such a blinding character that it leaves you with the expectation that there is no outlet other than to suppose that there is no "opportune future." And once more, being that you invite Me, and you know no soft corners from which to soar out of the vortex: the campaign waged to preserve You is no gimmick that Me here shoves upon you to be obedient to a serene state of knowing or existence that is not within your array of talents.

There is an existing body—what you seem to consider an antagonist—waging your Armageddon, which has as its calling to change your attainable and promising path. It is momentarily seen by you as a conquering blockade to the joy within, to your physical and mental agility, and to drawing intelligence from Our admired sectors that you have forever pined to become versed in. As you have earlier greeted this inhibitor as a separate force, you are not able to deny that this distinctiveness is what sets up your actual choice when you oppose hope, or more aptly, when you oppose Yourself. Keep open the avenue for this evidence to freely enter into your mind's vault of gems so that when the flash of a loss and no opportune future smashes you (and smashing is what Me here sees it to be), you have Our luminous surrogate of Hope's grace melting the thought form. This transmission was written in Your Ethereal coding notably for this circumspect investigation in which you participate. Yes, We agreed for you to become a visitor to "no opportune future" and to search and apply the corresponding Grace within You.

To doubt that you have already matched favorably where you once theorized you could not is another unsighted habit that is thrown at you by these artifices.

Savor the rapture as the former modes fade with your choice to be the decision maker where You opt for sweeps of favorable circumstances over smallness. Reexamine from previous days what glint of boldness conspired next to You when you industriously mined for Your authority and therefore the tools to overcome the fog. It was, when you pinpointed the energy of temporary chaos aflame with the fallacy of "regret" and there accessed the presence of the Figures emitting the ingenious remark that you are not less for any experience. THEY solicited you with the feasibility that all your participations are trainings without diminishment. Take this Providence and wield it when you stand in need of it.

There is a replica of me in my effort?

Very near in your recent past, these specialized Sources of Light intellect reinforced your efforts there in Terra when They caught sight of you wising up to the utter lack of relevance "regret" has and how it abducted you into a vagueness that, by default, there is no other choice except regretting. YOU, with Them, became the velocity rebuffing the doom of regret, and now, of "no opportune future." Still, take prudent note: no such united Velocity could have occurred with these Partners without them seeing you close by, which is a derivation of your willingness to defy. These universal solids are awed by your ravenous thirst to arrive at what you can be, unrestrained by any coercion equipped to shake your Star's invulnerable state.

I clean my Star to clear the path.

Your Co-Creators or Partners in competence assisting Us in your chosen studies here on Terra are poignant designs of moment. You migrate into Them with a mindset like Theirs and They, with commensurate or more force, are moved to assist you by dispatching Their finely correlated measures, with you as the supervisor to your promotion. You walk with Them and can dance with Them. THEIRS are inviolable oaths to you that are for only Their highest and best and yours. Ether essences, which are quantifiable with machinery that will be divulged someday, are enamored with the lengths you take to convert thoughts of you having a starved nature into the knowledge that you possess qualified features of universal proportions that are there for you to grow and know. THEIR eyes see no defeat. Likewise, Their arrival on your stage is to engender an amount of shock or uneasiness to alight your sights with the way to your crowning expression while in this carnal residence.

It is the drive of the guides in Ether form that are provoking you to recall your ambition to fuse with the many variants of your Star's castings.

37: ABUNDANCE IN DEPRIVATION

Certainly, the I in the sky hears the scream. However, the I in the sky admits that I have no access to circumstances through which to experience "abandonment," since my residence knows All to be one.

It is unmistakable who your associates are and your cry, "I am left alone!" You stifle your brighter smile inside. The deceivers have told you that these Beings found in the Lines of Love forsook you when you did not obtain the recent material of your desire. Thus, intrudes the division of memory loss, cutting you off from the never-failing scope of Our Affinities and Partners in competence, who are there to direct you into freer margins in which to administer your momentary experience. The misleading rationale pounces, that you are incomplete due to inability and the lack of a shiny gain. This commences your disassociation from the Ethereal team's prowess.

While your partners with Our Affinities are there for you with their ingenious revelations, they don't privilege you to sit idle in their arms.

It is Me who pummels you with scenarios laced with facts that are predicted to cause doubts to surface about you being the whole achiever that you wish to be. Your pretty object was not secured, and you doubt the powerful You of Our disclosures. Until you no longer hesitate to live the truth of your ability and the knowledge that You suffer no deficiency, the same circumstances will be born as necessary incitements to cajole you to search and find an undistorted image of the Self. Trapped in a device of Our making, you have the mechanism for extraction.

Ambushed!

The material scarcity will never immobilize you, but eventually it will be enough to cause your reactive mind to remain certain that you are an apt being when you see yourself as "deprived."

I question the Light of All for the truth to the way.

The way is to move in front of the shadow-self you shelter because you are afraid that you are this fearful shadow-shroud.

Not fatigued yet from punching the impenetrable wall of "deprivation?" Our staged circumstances return until you counterpoise them with the faith that you are acquainted with specially guided labor that is decisive to Your ends. Decide it will be at your disposal upon your call to action to Our Source within. Recognize the inner Capital that causes you to want for no greater resources. This is not a slighting of your pleas regarding practical concerns of materiality, of which you suppose you are being deprived. However, the prerequisite to subduing the thought bombardments takes priority. How else will you come to terms with your complete competence? You readily overlook the simplicity of the Way. You have shown that you do not search for Light functions in mastery without looking from the panorama of a hole that barely permits infusion of Light. The awesome ingredient to the story unfolding as you wish is what some refer to as faith, the healing thought that it is within You to advance as your visionary mind dictates. Do not misunderstand. WE do not agree to any precept that another being or person will rescue you. While you team up here and multidimensionally with others for your enterprise, the faith and action are upon You to rouse.

Accredit yourself as competent to be with all that is necessary to generate a fertile harvest, accentuating your best presence, and this will obviate the need We have to send more courses in deprivation. Dare to see this sight of You, and the key is not to tire from the heights. Accordingly, the door from which further studies are sent for you to experience a paucity in material resources will be locked. There also, you will assemble an accomplished energy resonance that grants your induction into a higher tone, and the shadow-self will leave for the semi-ethers.

It is not so that you have made any pact of poverty.

MY Terra twin does not like preaching. The anvil crashes.

Here is the transference by which you are best able to let it seep in: there is not merely a plan B out there for you to chart a winning course when you perceive that plan A is foreclosed. When your practice is to automatically put further thoughts of promising chances on top of foreclosed expectations, there will be no instance in-between for dalliances in fear. Nothing in between except plans B-Z. Infinite aptitudes remain in your hands after another one is forgone. Meaning, you suffer from no shortfall. You may be transitorily without your polished Earth treasure, but you are not in scarcity of the Wherewithal.

Again, My arrival in your now less-hollow shell was possible because you accept that, within your comprehension and capacity, innumerable strategies exist to fulfill the conditions you imagine to be requisite for enjoying all of Terra's charms. Precisely, while you do not have the exact shining object of your previous desire, you approve of what you do have as viable to happiness. Your frame of reference is broadened.

My prosperity lies in capacitating the Self, a Self I can't clearly gather in my intellect, though I somehow recollect pacing alongside with on occasion.

OUR mandate is for you to regain Your reserves in order to amplify Light so that you may not only spread this Light, but also enjoy Terra's many charms—as opposed to the objects you have previously set for acquisition, in which fear was the catalyst in your strategy to obtain them. When you substitute your trembling and in its place you implant intransigent ambitions to know only infinite opportunities, there will come the other compliments to your Being in Light, such as no urgency to indiscriminately clutch for objects with no verifiable traits outside of the material. Unquestionably, adequate solvency will come to meet your needs, along with those objects of whimsical comfort, only with differing brandings of importance.

Earth's college of creation ferments the by-product of fearless expressions of faith and assigns it to the Ethereal communities not defined by current definitions of disjointed time and space. By osmosis, the Ethereal occupants receive this vibrational nutrition. Stepping outside of linear time, you may even come to partake in the crop of your invention while you wittingly merge with Your co-participants. There will be no start or final point, solely a fusion with fractals of your Valor.

38: MIXING UP THE DESTINATIONS

It is Me who presses you as you curse Me for missed timetables you decided would correlate to the parameters you set in acquiring your pragmatic goal. The fiery red ball you throw at Me combats and severs Us.

Nonetheless, throughout the rage you leave feasible avenues for variant illustrations that are conducive for a healthy perceptivity to counter your deeply felt experience of "delay."

Meaning?

You are considering additional options that will please a grateful heart such as yours.

There can be no delay if all chances and circumstances that passed you by are not suited for Us.

Reconfigure the playing field.

Spot on. Frantic grasping to quicken the timetables is most certainly a digression that frustrates your making acquaintance with satisfactions that are superior to your narrowing and traditional comforts.

You have even elongated the window to adapt to an outcome that usurps the goal you once targeted; that is, if the end formerly plotted does not meet soundly with Our song of solidarity you are coming to know.

Without doubt, the I in the sky will affirm that there is no reason for a timetable or even for your practical and singular objectives. Your earlier-drawn endgame will be less your focal point when repositioned mindsets surface consequent to the additional spot removal from the brushing just gone by. During this very communication, a metamorphosis occurs as to the latitudes within your sights. It is an ongoing absorption by you of the application of Light that is causing your Earth self's identity to be uncomfortable with your Heart-Mind's takeover as the shepherd for learning of Our uninvestigated havens.

Perk up. The practical and predictable was never a fancy of yours. Engineering of Our merit is a final solution all in itself.

A diversity of subjects that We like and are partial to are coming into your imageries, still not altogether evident, but you will come to appreciate them as satisfying.

Since you have hidden in the recesses of other timelines the exquisite rapture of being totally occupied within a vortex of Light where you can only know stable reposes in beauty—beyond descriptions within the words of 3D—you give minimal effort to shifting from your culture's cushy ambitions you mistakenly believe to be a Nirvana.

Of course, until optimal synthesis of Light matter manages to saturate the Heart-Mind, all obligations that could solidify you into a future design with others have agreed to be put on hold, lest such connectors impede the projects of Ours.

Locked in a vortex of one pointless attainment and loss to the next!

WE are at the turn you made into the persuasively troubling thoughts you apply to solve your insecurity. Blaming the randomness of the universe, you open all the roads leading to chaos and strife.

The spaces you call universes operate within strictly tuned Codes, all of which guarantee unprecedented energetic artistry to arise out of your journey to "Self-love." Your pilgrimage allows You and the canvas of the All to become more prolific with your refined definitions of the Love you study.

Commanding your internal world of wonderment is the one and only circle you are certain to begin, and will finish.

You despise me because of Your conviction that you are plodding more sluggishly than in any recent memory, and without desired results. Your posted signs for progress are what were mislaid. There was a well-fortified whimsical force fueling you when you drove the pickets into your canvas. It was an energy of blurry compulsion possessing you to quell a deafening disquiet brought on by you accepting that you were vulnerable without societies' symbols of "security". Ripping them out of the ground without trusting that you will have satisfactory happiness with their replacements, you assume your plans to be pointless. There is no excitement from seeing yourself making headway with dreams more polished than those physical tokens that world culture celebrates.

All petty madness in clutching at random straws We are substituting by way of you agreeing to lovingly accept repositioned outlooks you soon will come to see as successes.

It is disconcerting because Our modified stick for approximating what is an "achievement" in your life has no longer any marks that give seniority to physical trappings.

The power to greet with a fresh, smiling face and the boldness of a "God" an obstacle you initially recognized as unbearable and avoid succumbing to the fear, even when pushed by the illusionists to escape into a "cushy" and practical end, is a consequence of unions you have made with the Capital of Affluence in the All. Your cooperative stance with the Lighter entities assures robust meetings with a prowess you have long forgotten.

Contentment is won at the end of my monetary victories. Point!

The onslaught of the dazing manias arrive for an encore with your commencement to withdrawal from admiring the inconsequential crazes reinforced by cultural norms. These infatuations you are abandoning were not of Our original setup. The fact that it is no longer a potential for you to block out Our fresh discoveries is lost on you because of your near panic stemming from the pragmatic codes of living that are being literally erased from the earthly you. You cannot shun the acuity that you no longer give precedence to procurements that contain no indelible traits.

A turbulent path of unknowns is your opinion of an earthly reality in which you agree to a guiding device that does not decree an image of Terra's mineral of gold as the choice subject of the journey.

Do you insist on your shortsighted "goal" and "timeliness" for grabbing your "gold" because you fear the path that holds maximums you are not sure are adequate for imparting lasting success? It is only your trivial occupations of a lower nature that are not sure. Because We are sure. The residue base manias inscribed in you are no larger than your memories.

Your completing trials that amount to sanctuaries in material gain is a warm and fuzzy cover that We have outgrown as Our main token of victory.

As you spread your visual orbit of rewarding exploits to include boosts out of energetic density, your Star loses the weight of material insecurity.

Presently, however, all that is to be your glory is crusted with fierce insistence at any cost to rapidly finalize your once-sought utilitarian conquest. This is your only salvation when your insight into your industriousness, and your conviction in the fact that all vital energetic and material attainments are accessible to you, have fallen into the saturating fog.

The road of appreciable heights unsteadies your earthly bearings.

Thunder from the unrecognizable rancors announce threats of material "shortfall" and hasten you toward an abrupt finish so that you may wedge yourself into the ordinary stations of success. Agreeing that there is harmony for you by paying heed to these intimidating noises shuns reconciliation with Our unabridged version. You will betray Me, your most excellent companion. This voice of Me exists to watch you mutating the figures of fear fantasy that grind at your Core into a trust of Self-love and worth.

It is You who are the founder of Our desirable reality of being sure-footed with strengths of universal Light that are shrewd enough to remove the dread of the unexplored and readily create anew.

Your usual verification of the credibility of my proposals is Our current juncture.

OUR prevailing conclusion: validation that your schemes were myopic, having little suitability to Our plan.

You hesitate with remaining doubt. Pay heed, all bids to deviate from Our arrangement to excel will be quashed.

39: SOOTHING REMEDIES

You recoil into the gaseous oblivion that you regularly descend within when you want to dodge the templates transported with You to Earth's plane. More accurately, they are not merely templates, but binding gales precipitated from your unrestrained passions when on similar Earth journeys. Some call it karma.

When facing your momentous cohort in this forthcoming exercise, mobilize your sympathetic tolerance. With this, you will soothe those winds and convene lines of regeneration that can wipe your accounts free. As you manage what will likely resemble startling rushes of animosity being thrown at you by your karmic cohort, have the sensitivity to appreciate that he suffers torment. This practice counteracts every tendency you may experience to dominate through entering into cycles of antagonism with this affiliate in your repositioning. When belittled by your karmic rival in the cyclone, or when the antagonist infuriates with deception, degradation, or physical assaults, while physical removal is your obligation and right, when you encounter the rage attune to the expanded range of your Being; give your reactive mind a respite and permit your Heart-Consciousness to step in with the understanding of their diseased ignorance that is manifested as hate.

Commonly, at first, you move close to this most unrelenting flame of hate, feeling instigated to quell the flare with your rage. Rather than act upon this, you transfer from your sovereignty of gentle understanding a wish for the other to be free from the pain brought on by their suffering with hostility. Moreover, you give life to a truth from the All, that behind their hate-filled misery lies the same unabashed beauty as found in all the components of creation.

When you practice offering from the most genuine part of your being the intent that your brother be free from torment and all its causes, without connectors to any expected return, denouncement, or anxiety for the outcome, you are the seeker at the Void. This featuring of your finest Self balances the scales and quiets the gales.

My causal gusts remain a mystery to me.

What started this encircling of me in these windy torrents of anger?

As We are overachievers, they are of tempest quality.

Then "We" should execute a steep and prompt ascent.

Plowing skywards in this course tenses every nerve. That Me up here proposes *taking the* meandering stairs or the scenic route.

Your answer as to what stimulated the onslaught of these tense upheavals is thwarted by your impacted excuses you make for why you do not see your hand as involved in creating the distaste you experience from your companion's raging behavior. You offer yourself uneducated labeling of your brother to avoid pinpointing your involvement in attracting this anger. This buffers simultaneous bids by your Brethren of Light to bond with your efforts so as to loosen the stranglehold on your Star. You declare:

- "I am just and fair."
- "This antagonist does not have a just heart."
- "They betrayed me."
- "They are the muck of the Earth, wanting to consume for their pleasure without regard for the havoc they reap."
- "Does it all really make any difference?"

Over and over, you bellow your repulsion for your partner in this exceptional study. No training in the mystical is a precondition to solve the rationale for their presence.

WE turn up at your Self-nurturing concession: You requisitioned this state of affairs that you believe are violations of your solemn foundations by your partner, friend, or relation so as to have this chance to pass the test in being merciful with yourself and your partner. There was a "tricky" switch you exposed when you distinguished that it was you and not your partner who was the name and the voice within the complex of your emotional repulsion as you vehemently reacted to the other's deeds. When your partner's traits repulsed you, you permitted yourself to receive the message of your part in molding this particular role in the present scenario. It was this which led you to forgive yourself for those same traits with which you previously operated.

Your impassioned descriptions of an "injustice" and "betrayal" are seen in the mirror of your making, which you only recently courageously looked into. It was a truth that the I in the sky could not have dredged up for you, despite your most frenzied begging. You engineered that puzzle, so you could be the fearless seeker who deciphered your "abhorrent" riddle with the only key—your willingness to take an honest and forgiving look into the image of you as no ingénue; you having attracted the conditions encircling you with acrimony. You were to be the exclusive healing agent by first having the audacity to look at all options and then admit that you brought on the tumult. It was you and not the I in the sky who could and did become the shining fledgling as you ceded that you, at another time and in another guise, decided to bring into your life this exact distaste you face, with the trust that when you eventually took a look at your part in gathering this hostility, you would not be trapped by hateful rivalry.

And so it was, that in the place of strife, you daringly opened up to the person who was in need of the reprieve—you. The reprieve was from the same so-called abhorrence that you previously inflicted.

It was your quantum leap out of the drab. Trusting yourself as a merciful force, you arched into placid orbits in the eye of your emotional cyclone.

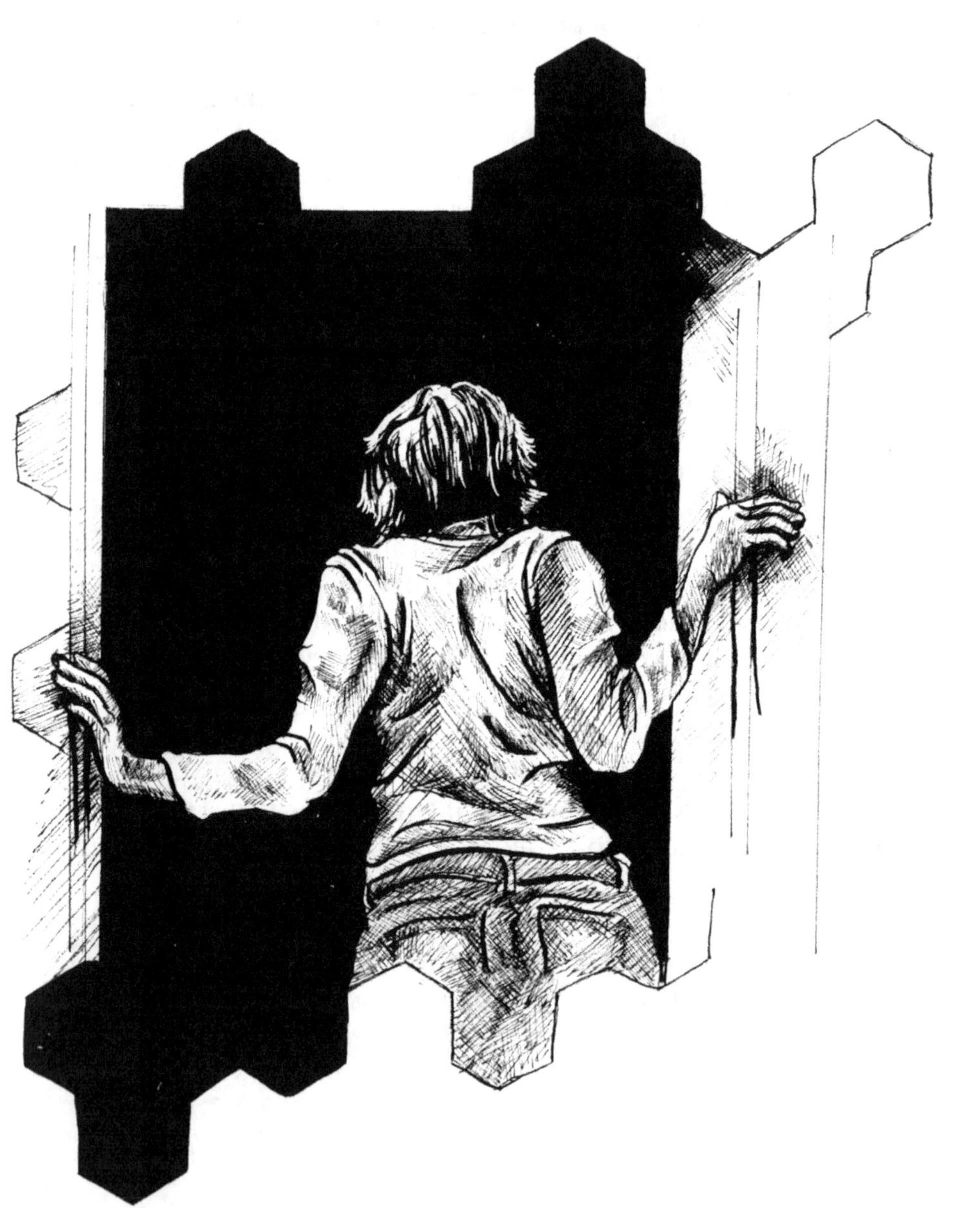

40: THE USE FOR THE FREEZING RAIN

Until this day, you were cagey enough to mute feedback from Me in reply to the deafening inquisitions you sent into the outer bounds. You wish to know the escape hatch but reject the door the I in the sky opens. Hence, the repetitious cycles of the "freezing rain" are Our forcible remarks, sent to you for the purpose of cutting into your resistance to addressing, with a bit of respect for accuracy, the subject you have been struggling to prevent from engrossing you. Fragmented details seep into your intellect. You dispute the source of this radical grime being pushed to the forefront of your consciousness by the increased oscillation of Light matter churning through your bodies.

Unquestionably, you are receiving the details quite accurately: Fiercely held and noble notions of loyalty to the high standards you have already lived and died for, such as happiness and justice for all, or even a theory of an "ideal," must never be erringly superimposed upon another as a reference point that you expect them to organize their conduct around. When these superlative expectations you pine to see from another or in an outcome from a scene you have sketched are projected onto these subjects or persons which are not in alignment to fully absorb the noble notions, only the most effective alarm delivered via what you refer to as "neurologically"—by way of your tactile senses—is sufficient to rectify your attachment to the delusion. Meet your friend who has greeted you with less force on other occasions: the "freezing rain."

Labeling with grand expectancy another human being as "the one" who has the earnest appetite to form a coalition with you to commit to any fundamental quest, including the mission of "love" for the sole purpose of the joy in the transfer, or to help free another of suffering and its causes, is a premise fraught with peril. When mistakenly arranged on a face attractive to your dull Earth senses, or placed upon an ideal reverie you have with finding "justice," it stiffens you into an assumption with no soft exits.

Nothing is real!

Your impression of this rushing and dreadful apprehension as having a physical component is not mistaken. Let the warm deluge of your intellectual receptivity to My information begin to thaw your sensation of the "freezing rain."

This sizeable upsurge of "Nothing is real" is Our design. How the I in the sky achingly monitors your episodes of "Nothing is real." Repeatedly, there is a dizzying discomfort in which, in a fractal of time, the mind is iced with a scorning intrusion: "NOTHING IS REAL."

The imposter fears!

The freezing rain of "Nothing is real" is not an imposter fear, but it is an entryway into your escape out of it, as well as your idyllic imposter formulas. It is possibly the closest you have come to the raw truth in a while. It can be likened to a Heart formation of shock, not fear from the illusionists. Still frozen, you do not ascertain the honest Heart of You to be the agency that forwards the cold bite.

The I in the sky exhorts you not to put off your reckoning with the clue entombed between valid memories and your wishful mirages of "what should be" the state of affairs you are enveloped in with this partner. It is not as though you have not seen the objective of the webs spun: of gifts at appropriate times, endless "favors," pledges of devotion to the same values you gladly gave your life for, guarantees that their presence was heaven-sent, the less than forward stance of soothing you by professing that they hold the only ticket for your entrance into the rooms which you comb the Earth to find. And then, there was the charade of offering you protection when you thought you required it but did not.

The earthly word you gave to be in virtuous sequence with this one who is supposedly diligent to your life's deep-seated vows muddies your head to a fact: their deliberately crafted actions and speech are not what you seek. A pining to walk with a fellow human while joined together with these flawless propositions is the glue you applied to superimpose "perfect" motives upon this collaborator.

Not once did you tolerate the question to surface of why it is this person that you specifically sought to hold dear your persuasions. You were sincere in your perusal, but why this individual?

When your well-correlated one professes unattached hopes of happiness for all, including you, while reminding you of how indispensable they are to your treasured project, you cannot bear to hear the perception that pleads for you to perk up your ears and listen. Their appetite has undisclosed leanings, and it is not for the conscientious models you craft.

While you have not been open to receive, the I in the sky is here to convey. WE have a need to be "deceived" so we may bring harmony to one of your energy fields. This is the blueprint suited to equaling Our lopsided scales through absorbing an earthly awareness of you in prior flesh, handing over your niceties with a motive that was less than apparent, but where you expressed a purity of "Love" you did not believe. You, having at an earlier place in time performed this act which is the equivalent to corrupting Love's constitution of kindness, We are obliged to encounter the same subterfuge as a recipient so as to repair the schism. And, until you dredge up your role as a counterpart in this reflection—which is moored in the daydream being illustrated for you—you will not be able to let go of this fictitious depiction to which you hold fast.

I abhor subterfuge. How could I possibly enter it!

Instead of digging for the implant that needs to be extracted, there you sit, shuddering because you have cut off all glimpses of facts that reproduce the truth.

WE have a frantic need for you to see the hypocrisy before you so that you can free Us from the panic and permit Us to resume positions more advisable for Our Being.

Know that what you have been watching is your partner skillfully encouraging you with the pretense of respecting the philosophies you extol and with the plan to enthrall not only you but your entire life.

Positively, We have elected an impressive balancing act that is well suited to dissipate the thick weight that you accumulated from unwise carryings-on in previous earthly composition.

Attain the dynamism to admit the inescapable facts. This empowerment We seek is found in knowing that you have within your mettle the means for commuting yourself and the other from what you fear are unfathomable transgressions, which you vaguely recall as feigning to another your commitment to a virtuous Love. This is where you will end the drastic ambush to your senses that comes from repressing knowledge of the accurate circumstances within which you persist.

Yes, in another place and time, you were in the opposite position. You were more of an expert at this deceptive game than the illusionist of your contemporary infatuation, and it was for the purpose of control and subjugation.

Giving too little credit to the healing power of loving yourself and the other by way of your gentle grant of a collective reprieve is a miscue that prompts you to look away every time you arrive straight at what are to you the "devastating" facts. You convert into harmlessness this harrowing conflict in which Our acquaintance is being subdued. Gibes from the shadow-seekers supervise you so that you don't accept the "unbearable" tale of the truth—that your inestimable Capital is devoted to an ideological partnership that is overloaded with your collaborator's duplicity. By coordinating your days around the hypocrisy and pretending that the state of facts you see is not there, you are a contributor to strife.

The convoluted excuses you dream up to dim your world when you are being jabbed with taunts of pretense by the partner induce your Heart-center to manufacture the shock of the cold freezing rain of "Nothing is real." Might it prove to be more explicit when the Heart screams, "This is not real!" You excuse this as a fake fear. Therefore, it is necessary to involve your tactile senses to crack the rock of your fantasy that the collaborator is deferential to your noble ideas. It is not possible for this component Vitality of your Star to tolerate you delivering its might into a partnership that is not sincere about the high-minded intentions it represents. The "rain" is its automatic washing mechanism.

In your present situation, the Star's concern is over-activated because you are expending its source seed, which is superior to all others: energetic Valor. This certain stock lies in reality-expanding thought imageries, such as compassion and justice for all, or in ideas of universal ideals, concepts that modernize the All. It is a mightily chased element. The Star uniformly conserves it from being consumed on an illusory project.

Acting as if you are in disbelief encourages what you seek; it is the calm in your daily rituals. And with this, instantaneously the cold chill of "Nothing is real" strikes you from your Center as being real.

Hear again, these infractions you refuse to believe are of your making. You, fearless one, called them up to heal similar transgressions of yours in another time and place.

Stricken once over, YOU MUST DECIDE. WE remain mired in Our efforts to discontinue your use of this Capital by way of your oblivious conjecture that you provide a most intrepid Valor to a partner who receives it with the importance suitable to its excellence.

Face directly that these are the winds of your gathering, accumulated when you dishonored the sincere expression of Love. Yes, when you professed that you had a benevolent heart, but in actuality, your preoccupation was to possess the mode of governing the other.

Amenable to the cues within the harrowing punches, you regroup by marshaling the ageless mineral of the spirit: acquiesce to the strength in forgiveness.

And being somewhat unwittingly stuck in this degradation, as many times in the past, the Star of You broadcasts loudly to your physical sensitivity this therapy that comports with Our edict to free

You from the clutches We once willingly agreed to be saddled with. "Nothing is real", shock compliance and is the most competent, the objective being efficiency.

I face my tumultuous disgrace in hypocrisy!

People climb through all weaves of fabric. Were you looking for mirrors to look into or doors to open? Retrieving precisely tuned instructions for your benefit, data that is buried deep in sadness avoidance, is not neat and tidy. We put on the spiked shoes for this incursion up Your icy cliff; just as at other times when you let your distaste for the genuine facts within which you persisted freeze you in time.

You have told your days of old. It was after confronting a desperation of the most oppressive nature that the light of your Star was able to compel you to flush out an especially fortified guard of your cave, which WE needed extracted. The sentinel to this den of yours was the one who oversees your life of habituated opinions. This imposter was unrelenting in announcing to your stagnant mind that all of the crucial judgments you have made during this stopover on Terra were not misguided. The I in the sky plays it back for you, the now of the escape, where—when hit with the mind-bending scare from "Nothing is real," you slung a large percentage of the imposter bodies from their encampment by pulling a learned relic from its exalted shelf: You suffer no debilitation or "loss" by admitting to being incorrect in one of your strongly held presumptive judgments or opinions, or by agreeing that you were once hurtful in your actions.

This concession facilitates the opening of the latch to your escape from heavy Self-deceptions.

It is correct that you incur no harm even if you are mistaken as to your favored and quintessential plans. It was in this realization that you could not be hurt by being "wrong" where you became attentive to seeing the simple information in the alarm, "Nothing is real."

As an opening to the closing act, your quintessential setup was not "real!"

You made an abrupt exit from all physical proximity to your partner, leaving universal themes for another time.

I mistook the sensation of "Nothing is real" as an insane paranoia, when in fact I shared nothing real with my partner?

History be told, that brought plan B, which were segments sure to inform you as to what your co-collaborator was dutiful. The inner You has an instinct for where there is false comfort, Our end-all indignation. Thus, the parade of appearances staged for your benefit showed no exemplary features of the kind you fantasized, only mockeries of the exemplary traits you celebrate. By consoling yourself with the intent to "Self-love", with the forthright recognition that you once contributed to the betrayal of Love's honest word, and then trusting the healing agent of forgiveness, you were able to send warmth and Light to thaw the freezing.

The motivator that attuned you with the truth was your remembrance that We pledged to never be obedient to an idea or a person that deranges you from spending your finite Earth time in optimal performance mode. The complete You is there to share with those many in your charge and waiting in the wings who dream to see you in your largest modes of Love to thy Self.

I am powerless to enjoy this Self-love when I am draining the Star's Valor in a fake enterprise. And what of this, a study in my missteps?

Your frame-up by the imposters managing you, the calamities such as "heartbroken" and "Why can't it be different," invaded when you identified realistic but unpleasant segments of your partnering. Numerous rupturing entities volunteered for this conspiracy cover-up to mask My voice and the actual countenance of the one you held dear. And, since you decided the principles you were fighting to live were the most excellent, you sustained support for the terror of your mind so that you could march on with your presumed joint quest. You judged this stance to be a prerequisite for upholding the fight to contribute your partnered Valor. The biting truth catapulted into your every nerve: "Nothing is real", was for you a fear to overcome so that you might continue your sanctified partnership. You were informed by the deceiving thought designs that this partnership of yours could be your classic dream. They hammered you with the controlling question, "Why can't it be different?", a variant of "It can be different" with this object of your infatuation. Those spellbinders are versed in barring you from any detail you surmise will bring on "sadness," "disappointment," or "regret." They played you by driving you to regard these words as having meaning to You.

The aftermath of this disorientation reigned as the "freezing rain."

The function of the Star's energetic Valor is not well served when you direct it to fall into a pit devoid of channels receptive to its dignity, either because you sent it to a person who lacks the conscious mind to respect its purpose or because you misjudged the project upon which you superimpose its force as an "ideal" undertaking for You, when it was not. When this is the predicament, the Provisions you garner from the Source to extend Love of Self and others do not find a compatible harboring station. In this case, the Star misses its mission to accent all it contacts as a remedy to clear despondencies born from the many varieties of fear. Because, if the intended recipient of this Valor does not authentically welcome the brilliant depths of its theme, or if the enterprise is not compatible with Our purpose, it will have no breeding ground to infiltrate as a nutrient for reconstructing the lands of pain into an archetypical bliss—which is its cardinal charge.

The stamina you used to summon the Valor occupied your Earth time; yes, in a fake enterprise. To prevent this, the Star's preservation procedure is perpetually set to "caution" for any such distorted conclusions. Transparent environs are Our desired positioning while here.

The dizzying electric shock was Our first choice when you found yourself in the depths. The I in the sky need not remind you of the other histories in which you superimposed non-existent motives, or non-existent contributions to Us, on other inappropriate targets. The Star's elixir describes for you all the malignant connectors to your earthly frame that need to be dislodged. Your Star, the architect of "Nothing is real," sends unpleasant waves to the mislaid dots. Your battle not to disrupt the warm and fuzzies with your partner cannot equal the fix of the piercing numbing that emanates from Our Star when you wallow in Self-deception. The Heart pulls into awareness the faulty lines so that you may decompose them with the Love you give to Yourself by severing your chains to the fake enterprise.

Had you been clever enough to repress the freezing rain, the flesh would have absorbed the diseased state of your fantasy. This was not to be your future. You rescued this Stamina so as to shift it to contacts and relations with projects borne from the spirals of Light-Love energy, waiting to meet it with a welcoming equal to its cause.

This sovereign clout of intelligent Light Love is the arbiter of all truths inherent in the process of life's evolution, no matter what grouping you wish to give to what you study. Should it be misreading a person's earnestness about edicts to live by or awarding deference to a state of affairs due not to their truth to You, but instead because you hunger for a fantasy within which to submerge your coherence, the purging eraser will follow. The list of the origins of the unnerving jarring is as diverse as your miscalculations, which may suffocate your Star and stunt your shine.

41: A PILLAR STANDS

Seasons stretching behind, a vow still rings in the Expanse, that you govern your transits in tandem with the Star's tenacious inspection before making any conclusions of word, voice, or judgment.

PART VII: VARIED PANORAMAS

42: LIMITATIONS OF YOUR LIGHT BROTHERS?

A derivative of Our clarifying your resonance on Terra was to unbind Your currents of endurance from the underbelly of the imposters to the level where their intrusions are barely a noticeable affront to making headway with Light genius. With this preparation comes the first chance to not literally clutch to what you see as the forces "above," and helpers from "above", or "beyond." You stuck to labels of "helpers" from "above" as a reliant armament with the assumption that they held your clearance into the Yonder lands.

Take the next move. Question whether these groupings need revision. Such carvings of thought can evince insights into the multidimensional You if you remold and reorganize the divides a bit.

I am testing whether my panoramas are all that more varied. Admittedly, while I do not see all the peripheries unambiguously, I suppose they are. Do these heavenly Light bands—whether brothers or sisters from above and beyond that have a presence in a particular sort of Light derivation—do they not have the freedom to serve and lead with free choice? And if so, from what set of options? Is their array of universal capacities as plentiful as mine?

All roads being paved with unconditional love, no destination is any less than the other.

My question not answered.

Persisting here in your substances of earth, air, fire, and water, simultaneous with the most dynamic proliferation of imposters in the galaxies, is every initiative which We contend is a sign of desirability.

I hear it: Coincident with the amount of thickness where I glide I have occasion to arise. My questions are not answered!

Yes, but the query was sent—and to the Source that at times sends the answers to one as headstrong as you in a manner that, if you are not prepared, will knock your earthly base.

Back to the point. The Light adepts have no primitive elaborations like yours to invigorate Them while they are in 3D shape to produce an output from thought, action, and emotion that has the might to reconstitute diversified energy sludge. Their actions are governed by edicts that will only distract your monkey mind from felling the crucial illusions we presently work to disband.

These edicts concern my passages?

The explanations will become germane only as you bridge into energy sectors that involve these canons.

My question is evaded.

The I in the Sky bathes in the rare colored lusters my Earth twin throws while you reposition your mind and agree to My bidding to refresh your awareness with further inquisitions into Our nature, all while positioned within these physical variables of formidable and confining potential.

Sketching myself behind the wheel of transport, quickened with Light and having this brother in Light as the co-pilot, all that I disperse surpasses my peaks and shades those of my previous focus.

43: FLUX AND NEW ADDITIONS

Those that I currently refer to as "others", yet at previous moments I had a need to cherish, were never meant to have an influence any greater than unknowable wanderers, coming and going, not viable for continuing with my newly charted exploits.

The gap from Our Star's earlier renovation is wide enough that you have had time to settle securely in the maxim that deems flux and mobility as required for accessing the insightful information to be gleaned from a more transparent Star. In this circumstance the flux was the casualty to your expectation that a certain person will be present at your side during pivotal junctures in your days to come. You have let the "dear" ones go to their individualized endearments, where they will augment their own Affinities with the Graces. Your thoughts of late of the previous "partner" as an ill-defined other should reassure you that the person was not in proper configuration with the next course that We have arranged. No "loss" is held within your emotional inscription observed by the I in the sky. Auspicious bridges unrelated to this "other" delineate for your forays.

The idea of coldness in your heart falls away as you deem it a sensory error, a speck swept from your slate to clear your path. Your anticipation of a kind of optimism peeks in as an intuition. The thoroughfare for new arrivals commences. You trust you will have others fastened you to Terra.

The excursionists (as are all Earth beings are) turn up: flying, playing, intriguing, poking, elucidating, scheming, simply standing in wait, coming and going, some without a shred left of the appearance you knew them to have in past embodiment. Reliably, they deliver the scope of achievable affairs for you to choose those that you permit to affect you and with what details. In this contribution of presences is your freedom as to:

- Which person you will allow to take
- Which can give, teach, elude, or delude
- Which to love
- Who you will receive love from
- Who you will inspire to heal
- Who will give pain, and who will take it away
- Who will settle you or let you soar from all earthly gain.

And, yes, you will show your partiality for those who will bring despair and those liberating you from its darkness. You may take upon your travels explorers, one for each educational discipline. The favorite for your learning, heavy or light, is part of your right. Our time-tested mantra, the mentality of forgiveness and compassion is trustworthy for composing the Light.

Should one or all prove to be drifters who oppose Our energetic synchrony, the shiny contrast from your Illuminator escorts you to where the sluggishness festers, if you dare to look.

44: HIGHER GROUND

You were not accurate in trusting that the emotional finale with your ex-planning partner was the "freezing rain." In this Now, you have traversed the tightrope over the final divide that was predicted to decisively disjoin you from the trappings of your karmic planning partner/former Earth associate. Your queries are answered. The otherworldly plan you agreed to with the ex-partner did immerse you into viable expectations that you had every intention to achieve. You envisage this formerly arranged forecast as an eerie scene from some forgotten past.

Your next level of altitude is ingesting shame's cure. Recede from blame you leave apportioned upon thy Self along with some to the other. When you retreated from a former deal of this sort with interest in corrective results for you both, and with the wish that you both mature into your very best, you invented the Light stock of absolution. The fluidity of this thought product proffers as a discernment that you will contact as a sanctuary in your future.

Disentangling from formerly set courses for travels, permanence, loyalties, partnerships, missions, shared goals, grounding forces, and financial exchanges with individuals or group members with whom you had worked out plans and ends at that other fair place in time frees for you avenues containing schematics in countless other expeditions. This turnabout from your projects should not be accompanied with feelings of either harmful or helpful. Those you call family, and others you don't, came into this temporary expression with outlooks about you that were concluded in a more ideal place for comprehending a typical path to an end that both of you sought. Likewise, you did the same with them. Covenants with these group members were part of the monumental project that was broadcast in a region and in a span nearby this one, where nothing cracks.

Bring a keen eye to the many explanations for your life. You have agreed to show love to all those who tug at your emotions and breathe life into your spirit so as to hike up a degree their responsive perspectives correlating to their growth and yours.

You pause momentarily, realizing that your better sense has taken from you all predictions you made that you would any longer show and receive "love" with this other of your cosmic arrangements.

Your recounting of this history is true. The precursor to permitting gentle exit from the heavenly design was to stand yourself beside your Etheric co-designer and demonstrate your willingness to love, if allowed, with no need to receive. This was the way to abatement of historical energies that could make strife your life. In your every word and thought, you upheld a Self-autonomous tenderness in response to the rages thrown at you. The expression your sister received from You, as intended, was a mental embrace of caring. From not one taunt directed at you did you feel you wanted to reap any form of return or throw insult. The Light pillar of this gentleness mended any frequency that was not harmonized between you and the ex-partner, and you and Yourself.

Conceive of this with Me: there was a pasture where you toiled with a sweet swelling in your heart to do the right thing for one whom you have taken responsibility for or for those you decided needed your attention. The enthusiastic buildup you produced in this pasture beguiled these beings set to receive your especially crafted bounty, for them to accept or reject. The illustrious supplies of Love you spread before these wonderful souls furnished a retreat in loving sustenance to all those who were willing to join. Your provisions alleviated any rough energies that held a propensity to ruffle you.

Hold on in this reminiscence.

These beings were to be crucial to memorable chapters in your visit to Earth. They were to define how you would fulfill your program to honor love. However, should there be no balance for all parties' growth in the final blend of motives these leagues should be made obsolete so that others can re-structure. Your circumspection by the Light began the erasure process of all bonds that were inconsistent with Our concordance. Unquestionably, this was sanctioned by Our authority.

And, be it indispensable to your loving role, you will observe the will of the planning partner to leave the plot as a sign of respect and love for them, as they turn to auxiliary stages of their interest. Yes, the lines to be written in the stories to unfold with your formerly avowed practicing partner are written not necessarily from the ancient vows, but from the shifts out of the vow taken by you and your brother or sister. There is no loss to you so long as, at the time of their flight, you were mobilizing your finest integrity with the anticipation of sharing it where needed. Brothers and sisters to come will know this esteem.

It is so. Alarming histories are brought to your dexterous Earth dance. Dancing with reflections upon reflections that cast images for you, but those for which We don't await. These heritages are readily set to the side without consequence merely by Your wish for happiness and the causes of happiness for all who have left, no matter the "wrongful" circumstances, and for them to be free from the causes of suffering. The birthplace of this sentiment is not of the mind. You trigger this benefaction from the Heart's resplendence. There will be no guessing the place of your aspiration when a picture of your dance partner, who has bowed out, is captured in your sights as a being towering with new contentments, and accordingly you find yourself blessing this departure with impartiality and tolerance.

I have great doubt that my world is not diminished in this process.

Yes, the depiction of You as a meaningless happenstance staggers your gait. Conjectures picked up from the lower realms attach you to the belief that you are made small without the partner who offends you or brings you opportunity to offend. Nowhere in the benevolent universe of You is there even a light breeze from the laws of cause and effect which mandate the harm of wrongs that infringe upon Our energetic vitality in order to restore equity. Make this distinction: Your Sovereignty, which is maintained through sustaining the integrity of the Self's energetic containment field, is incapable of pledging or being subject to diminishment or infringement if We are to abide by the universal laws of evolution. It is the order of these Rules that You remain intact. Tolerating abuse is a fracture. Ergo, when you surrender yourself to personal offenses, it is not possible for you to demonstrate an authentic healing Love for yourself or another from your Star center. For, with this submission you distribute shares of You. Those once preordained to turn up so as to even out past circumstances are to never weaken Your Star's distant sweep.

That certain "truth" of the essential nature of suffering, which by the default of lack of information you chose or acquiesced to, had seductive wrappings meant to change its hue to transparency according to your willingness to see the helpfulness to You of that which charms, that which harms, and that which heals.

45: ALLIES FOR GOODBYES

Another weighty grip has eased. Your Self-navigated Star sauntered through the bounty of your mind, comparable to sailing inside the fog with a reforming outlook, rooting out all matter that was hiding the ideas that seated you in lethargy, while not sensing anything good or bad, or pretty or unpretty about each and every of these dormant distributions of thickness. From Your apt estimate of the facts you were living came the heralding of the turning of the page. Cutting away or helping another to do so is one of the most profound gestures of love you can dispatch to the one with the mistaken opinion that you are a necessary presence in their passages through the stages to come. Without concluding any errors for either of you, there is a sweetness for you when you envision the mending tone of not feeding the hollow inflection on your side of the correspondence with your brother or sister. A nod of pardon and release makes way for differing thruways of gainful correspondence for both. A reckoning burden can be earned should you not depart, thereby facilitating the partner to miss occasions intended for his maturation.

Likewise, discontinuing to roost at their side should be your move for the sake of unburdening your partner when stagnation in heaviness is sensed, which neither you nor your partner is willing to cure. And as your decision will dictate, there will come those to add wind to your flight. Be vigilant and there will never be an oversight as to the specific strain that requires removal. Should you set your mind's aim there, severing ties can mobilize scenes hibernating for you that will outperform the ones you predicted with those with whom you have cut the association.

I am overwhelmed with nostalgic unease. Is it that I gave enough before ending this course?

This is the last fiber in your meticulous review. No leaving is premature after you have sighted the uncompromising pressures either of you or both of you are hoisting upon the other and your role in shaping the deeds that occupy your emotions. And then, deliberating there with your mending Graces, you place the seal to prevent new entreaties from the other or from you into these dissolving ties. The door of next onset would not be there had you not landed squarely within this specially crafted looking glass and confirmed the closing.

46: LARGER VIEW OF THE THIN LINE

Your usual digression in the entertainment you have pleased yourself with is finished. Now, you are deposited with the I in the sky. The train tracks for your march onward, left waiting as the warm and fuzzies enveloped you, were reworked after your visits to the margins of Our trails. Nonetheless, others await Our scenic tour.

The drifting into fanciful flights are chimes in your mind that curtail tributes to Your peaks and eventually reveal capped extents you at first did not acknowledge. Everything and person that averts concurrence with Us will be ejected from directing your setting, with more or less disarray, meted out by the typography upon which you have installed your roads. And, yes, should you not stride in debris-free scenarios, the expunging crew awaits to shove you into linkages covered with the sheen of the Creator of Light.

My walk is closed and narrow.

Refined implementations of You are a sort of narrowing and at the same time a tightening into a groundwork of fitness and distinction that prepares you to widen into the unimaginable, not fully believed to exist, but of which you have been getting flashes of the message. Shedding burdens during the exercises in expansion makes the avenue lighter to tread. Unveiling attainable bounties is not won through mere thought, as once was the case when the Soul was manifested without its current physicality in one of its long-forgotten trips through Terra. Physically acting to shed that which loads you down in thickness is a prerequisite. This includes these others, material and Ethereal, who affect your dormancy. The surface, seemingly a slender place from which to fall, is a foretold aversion because you have not frequented this land with its many mystifying and intricate wanderings that keep one above the fray. The byways are thin due to universal edicts and keystones that sanction only your walks and thoughts which are exemplars of goodness to Yourself. These channels are well stocked with myriads of telling distinctions to show you how to arrive at unmapped highlights within. The slimming-down sensation is a temporary ideation, until you see Your motion's grandeur.

The subordinate slopes of the path, referred to as the sideshow, have never been of Our dominate interest as the source to strengthening Our domain.

Musings of certain souls often show up in the margins of your illuminated stretch and there sow seeds of clouds, thus dimming the lights. They plead with you to return to your romp with them. This one jaunt you now return from, surely it was dim and wholly devoid of My presence. These sideshows in which you partook with every sense were the bulk of your life until your Star's translucence quelled their drags, sidelining them to the fringe.

Surprise! You are learning how to walk again, and in a different kind of gait, and so much later than the first time. This walk is by and through all that detracts and averts you from being compassionate to Your primordial poise among the Stars.

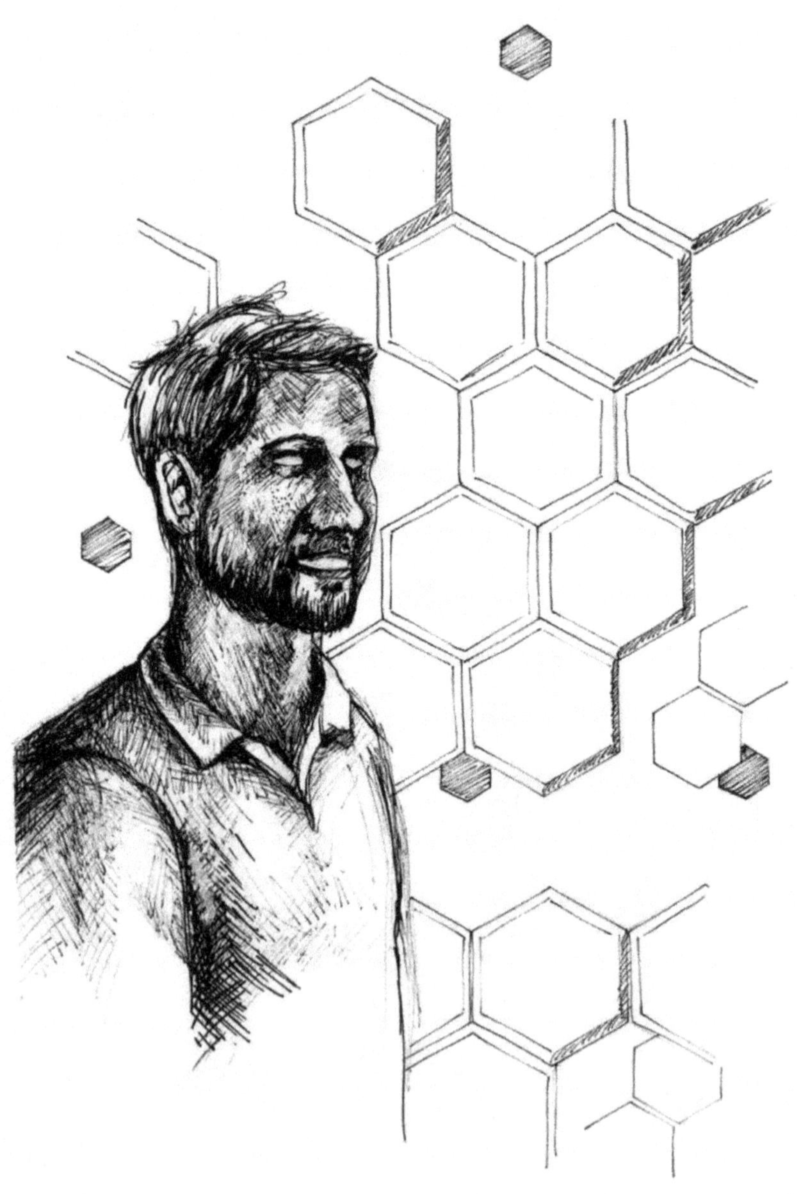

47: SEEING INTO MY CLEARER MIRROR

You look back upon the affronts of the "freezing rain." You are sure this cure to your paralysis was a necessary measure to route you away from the tracks you shared with partners whom you also once chose, both those of benevolent Light and those of Earth. Your abiding belief in the desirability of the withdrawal from these liberated companions has convened substitute, to-be partners.

Attached attitudes of my latest mate need to evacuate from me, for they relentlessly jab me with their plans for coming along to my future.

The unwavering decision you made to continue beyond the horizon of the former ones need not be composed from furry. A genial espousing of your alternative vistas is more than an adequate solvent.

You admire new roads, though suspicion breeds in you that these earlier collaborators have not withdrawn their taunts of trying to bring you to coordinate with their course, a course that has become outdated for you. Have you become wise to the precise identity of the force that seemingly calls you back to these dated plans?

I want distance from all who come at me with wrenching restraints. These pacts were rendered inconsequential through my choice or, if you prefer, the decision of my vanished partner in the pact. It is counterproductive for them to stall me with any attempt to rule me with their ways.

You debate Me as to whether the workings of an ex-Ethereal or ex-earthly associate can stall what you are seeing as your newly gathered and accelerating force.

I hurl them to sail away, any of those connections to former associates, whether beheld with my eyes and ears or noticed with my other talents. My wings will never again be clipped. Any creature, heavenly or low, who crosses my boundary with narrowing advice or rigidity—I detach them to pursue their own vocations. It will be my doing to have a safe space from all of those I previously joined with in these antiquated projects.

Each Light helper and healer once pertinent to my vanquished pact—what is the truth of their range or competencies? From the grappling dragging me, I'd say they have a bias for the plan I rejected and are hanging onto to at least my emotional bodies. Is this a reminder of their unconditional supervision of me, which I invited a way back?

Even know dejected by you, the co-mixtures you built in these earlier phases creep along with you.

I call to the very Light which established All to fully eradicate from me outmoded ties that do not support my reversals. I am the purging storm, blowing away from me whatever is bent on overlaying blocks upon my command. Celestials or other entities tampering with me, with a multitude of configurations left for them, would do well to serve another. Do they retain the dynamism to renounce their taunts which I discard, or are they like an old Earth friend backing a fantasy, since that is all they know?

Roots of suspicion and fear in your somewhat arbitrary thoughts are tripping up your climb. When you denounce those you were tied to with mistrust, carrying the weight of condemnation, you open to disarray.

I am trying to disengage clutches that are not there?

The persuasion hitting you—that you are inept—brings you to suppose that you do not have the traits necessary to evade unrecognized clutches, which are admittedly somewhat more than a fantasy. Although, whose grasp do you seek to escape? It is not the pointed claws, but your judgment that you have not the skill to release them that bothers you. Your pitfall is a sluggish intellect in not pinpointing what it is you encounter. While you imagine that agitations contain messages from the emotional body of an ex-relation, you are blinded as to where the primary vexing begins.

Visceral advisement sent from Me to transport You out of the morass have not been successfully pushed through the portion of your deliberate mind that screens instinctive impulses for final approval. The Heart-Mind does not receive the instruction. So, for purposes of your immediate notice, strenuous thrusts are sent, the author of which you presently have not identified. They suggest to you that the person you want left behind should not be left behind because of their favorable influence on your "higher path" for the "greater good" and because they are a part of the road to fortunate circumstances. It is Our safe bet that you will not ignore these irritants until you have vanquished them. Less noticeable hints are infused by the partner left behind.

The mantra I hear, which is that the person should stay for my "better good," does not have as its outset my Star's divining. This is the giveaway that the "better good" will give me away. Not favorable in any way!

These instigations of the "better good" have qualities that argue they are more than my mind's inventions, that they arrived from a Being with mental agilities above mine.

You are testing the waters. Have the bravery to see into the farther calling.

I was meant to reject a component of my higher existence, and its advice? The I in the sky is endorsing proposals I don't want!

To be more explicit, a somewhat "alive" version of you, a pre-dated relic with greater vibrational inhibitors, was left behind by the newly resonating you, and it over and again haunts and besieges you so that you don't outrival its version of you. What was left behind was a trajectory that is not in symmetry with Us after your choice placed you in the new amplifications We represent.

This annoys me nearly as much as broken glass scratching my Core.

These mental assaults from such an energetic body are part of an essential process that is coincident with your decisions for Our growth; they are there for you to use and refuse. And there, then, to glide into Your additional space. A Lighter body variant of your previous self does what it will to cajole you into finalizing the earlier dusting of your Star, prematurely or not, or to reenter the body's complexion. At this instance, your earlier variant is without consequence to all of your bodies. Your path can be permanently presented clear of this annoying pseudo simile of you, and thereby lay the thoroughfare for the rising of your ennobled voice. Albeit, you can always return to the so-called "better good" and the previous conditions with your cohort.

Each signaling, even if from one you suppose overshadows Your intelligence from the Yonder lands, shall be subjected to your test. You are waylaid by this screaming harassment: "Rejoin outdated energetic schematics of you for the 'better good.'" Giving respect to the idea that you should exist in a circumstance for the "better good", no matter the cost to You, invites strife. Insistences slamming your Lighter composition yelled that the sole road to happiness was filled with people who bring the "better good", and unrest. WE never meant you to choose such, but decide why you should be open to removing your previous version's onslaughts, which are trying to overshadow your renovated operational design. Faithfulness to the "better good" has plenty of room to ripen in your Heart when you decide it is for the maximal actualization for Our Earth you.

You were persuaded that the guiding directors of Our Ethereal partnership were callous. These were the very same entities who wanted you to follow what you hold in honorable regard as universal laws that escort the Soul into freedom. You deduced the paradox, that these same presences in Light were directing you to go back to the same partnership with the one who then had an aimless thirst to dominate and occupy certain sectors of your Star. At best, it is a confusing parable to confront.

Seeing that it was partially Our pre-dated relic that delivered the annoyances that led you to throw to the outskirts this former version of you, how does your guiding Light portray these differing portraits of You?

Empowered, with fewer manacles and moving forward is my modern portrayal.

While these invitations to the "greater good" were not adaptable to the Soul's serenity, there was no cruelty involved. They were pictorials mocking You for the well calculated expectation of opening your eyes to a permanent strategy for ending the impact of a misplaced brick in your book of logic: that these prior partners, Ethereal and earthbound—and their suggestions—were the sole pavers to your coming triumphs. That was the viewpoint you buried deep. It vied to keep you occupied and joyless.

Deciding there are exclusivities as to the paths leading to your happiness, or having the opinion that you should exist for the "greater good", are aberrations that obstruct your happiness. Bowing to the "greater good" in this circumstance threatened to shackle you with disorder. OUR quest for the "greater good" will be unmistakably heartening, and without onerous chaos.

The unease of failing to meet your long-sought ends, which came with your envisioning the personage of strife leaving your "epitomized" world, was sure to transition into tranquility with the shift of your imagery a slight notch into the additional multitude of advantages you have to claim.

Accusations of fraud and incompetence against the Lighter-bodied directors were predictable. As yet, it is not possible for you to distinguish between the prior simile of your vibrational body and that of a Light being.

Your Star awards no deference to another's supposed license to dispense a revered source of clarity, whether you perceive the source imparting it to be high or low. Opinions are crafted by both the Celestial and entities with lesser vibrational resonance.

You recovered Your Star's mapping agent when you became aware that chopping off many other bountiful passages for moving into Our composure and your good fortune because you exalt a person, idea, or object to be mandatory to your singular path—even if the topic is lofty—slims your resources for constructive guidance down to a lifelessness.

WE chose the broader options for Us. This decision to leave behind the discord was enforced upon you by way of My utterance of the mental thought you picked up on. It spoke of your life as experienced in a tunnel, a notion We predicted that the inventiveness of your earthly Star would rebuff.

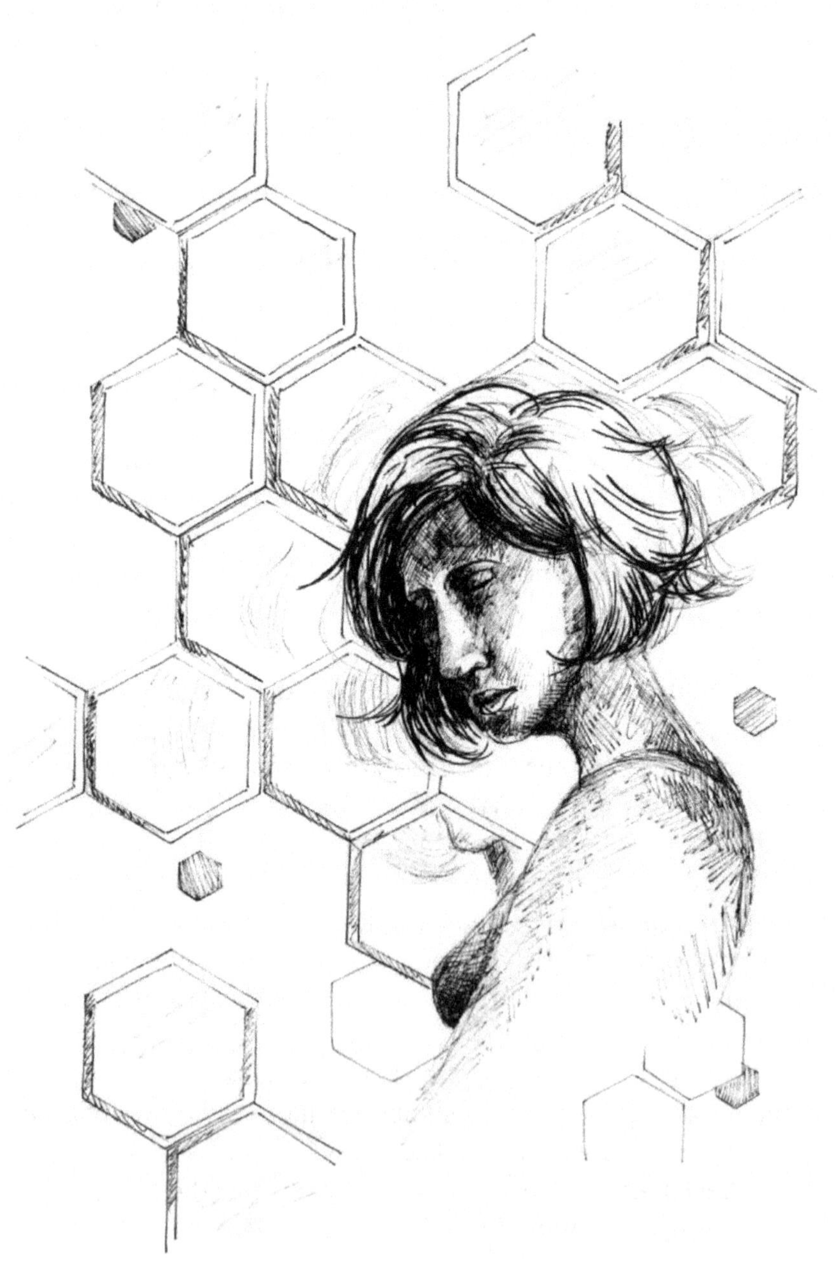

48: SMOOTHER GLIDING

The flair of Your soft countenance when faced with settings you labeled as threatening only a step previous to your sturdy resting spot is your profit from tailoring your lifelong beliefs to exclude certain cumbersome ideations that were matted to the Star's fluidity. Arriving unwearied and closer to the peak of Your mount proves to you a buzz that you were unaware of earlier than this place of Now. You have little reservation in your appraisal that the ingredient for your newfound working lies not in Earth's warm and fuzzies. You have honed your destination to tap into a landing constructed from a mysterious genius behind the panels of the warm and fuzzies.

In back of these planks I have located further staging arenas. They are of great interest to me. I see my wings will be accommodated within these spans.

You envision an unlived exuberance, but cannot possibly know its properties. However, because you have opened sufficiently to acquire a taste of its existence you have every reason to seek it.

My appearance is established within the Graces' malleable mix, and I will slide comfortably into anatomical Light intelligence.

49: THE FUTURE

There is no point in foretelling the future. Your familiarity with the most probable eventuality that exists at the time you are instructed on this forecasted event disconnects aspects of you from the Earth plane, which We both know is less than optimal. There, you flop about and forget the task at hand. This daydream turns you away from practicing the use of your Star and from setting your own extensions of how high you decide to rise outside of these divinations of another. When you feel that the corner would be better rounded by peeking into a window into the eventual, you miss the prize of the potential in the Now. If you were to have a foretold fate then effervescence's competent, hope, could not be endowed with its body.

PART VIII: HOPE'S FREEDOM

50: DO THE RIGHT THING FOR YOU

Involvement in the pains of a fledgling co-wanderer stall you. Doing the right thing most certainly means doing the right thing for You when you are overcome by the facade that it is kind to give from a sense of appeasement pity. This way of dispensing offerings in "kindness" is of no import to the other. Devoutness to another's pain, in this case the pleas of your brother, hold you accountable for encouraging the pain. Any twist of pity has ingrained the chord that you are more transcended than your brother. This ties you to a pain that is not yours. Before you is the day when you will wake up your lifelong friend, who is forever beside you entreating you to take hold of its outstretched palm. In this palm is situated despair's corresponding Grace, which is Hope's freedom. Eternal is its reverberation from the Source's endowments as an affirmation of gladness in a reassuring love of infinite renewal that has the supremacy of prospering when everything you assume can break has crumbled. It was your ingenuity in planting poppies in the darkness of a barren Earth by repudiating that which could be presumed as "wasted," and sending to this "desolation" a bright red horizon of the visions of Our inexhaustible Star, if only by having no remorse in rejecting another's impoverishment.

Their perceptual illusions are not of your doing. Do not contemplate a lesson in the sorrow of another, other than the practice of detached sensitivity that they are suffering from the delusion of anguish. While supplying kindness and good will to your brother or sister is a fine offering, bring caution and circumspection. Let no part of You sit in their bleakness when aiding them. And if your return to this other is sought through his pain, planted for your liking, know that there can be no recoiling to anything more than the myth of misery, clutching without caring whom it touches. Hope resides in observing all of life as a gift and a good fortune in which desolation is seen only when there is divergence from the realms of Hope's influence; that is, where the mind creates a rift of despair that obstructs your receipt of language from the Star advising you of the indestructible resource of joy.

Despair's ruination has gravity when it is spirited into your life via seeing your brother as defeated.

Held within the restraining curbs of sorrow's vacillating orbs you are sharing with a novice wanderer, You aspire for more.

51: BUDDING IMPETUS

I am battered and worn. What is undeniable are my failures in judgment! The rashness accompanying me on all my days here was no different than a razor slicing me from the one you call Me. YOU, never ceased, did You, in arranging curative themes on the cusp of my thinking throughout eras I have forgotten?

The lofty character of "discernment" is a propensity you have that is slumbering amidst certain covers. Is there really any question why this gift is left unwrapped? Look back and isolate the way that governed the bulk of your accomplishments throughout all your days here on Terra: the warm and fuzzies and culturally elegant pleasures. The route to them was as effortless as agreeing to partake in one of their standing invitations. The threshold was simple and subtle, a recognition that the recreations existed was the permit for descent into their shell.

This solves any doubt about their bearing in my life. Their undemanding access surely means a decaying desert as opposite my Star.

A sort of cerebral opulence will arrange the weave crucial to conversing with your Star's savvy so that you can render transparent the meaning, intent, value, and direction in any given state of affairs you encounter. Judging from the existing firmness of your will expect to live this Gift. When I say it is a Gift, I mean it is somewhat of an encoding in Your Ethereal DNA, which with a hardy resolve, is yours to unlock.

Repeatedly cornered in confusion, I grasp like a child.

The conundrum, by virtue of the fact that you have not persevered without fail when you strive to partner with the multi-level species of Light competency, you discount the plausibility of this relational network to sharpen your world. Your drive to arise from the ashes is obliterated by the Earth plane's thick and defeating energies. Gaining access to your hidden skills by way of intimacies with the Light adepts is an artistry unique to you on this go around. You must incentivize travels within this thin line by stoking an imagery of the fulfillments brought by the Grace of Self-love—actual tools to create not only joy but the material enjoyments that will complement Us. Expressions of Self-love grow your competencies. You must forever abandon the imagery that these instruments of mastery, emerging from your thoughts and actions that display Our best presence here on Terra, are merely surreal and unattainable. Again, agilities of mind, body, and spirit—obtainable by you—are quantifiable matter that does not dissipate. They are as real as the hammer is to the nail at the moment of its use.

When you weigh even momentarily the notion of the Grace of Self-love as a medium to deliver you from the martyrdoms, they begin to speak with a steadfast obedience to you. Give approval to their Voice, their palatial headquarters, to free you from the thunderous bells of the anti-You and into their curative properties. So that you may produce the joy and resources We aspire to, attune to the Voice heralding your mastery. This speech of goodness to Yourself will pacify the sounds of coercions that are deadening your higher senses with their shots of disorientation and grief. The astral brutes are entreating with proposals of remedies of control and frenzied graspings that you surmise are effective to protect a you that is illusory from hate, from hurt, and from material "deficiencies".

Admittedly, at this time the tools of the Graces are not simple to access because of certain specific pressures you permit to cloud your Star.

It is when you reminisce with this gladness in a reassuring Love of infinite intelligence and renewal that it begins—a companionship with your Lighter mental, emotional, and physical bodies.

The I in the sky calls forth how it came about that you were there, planting poppies in the barren earth by unlocking the door to the sight of a sunrise behind the aching fear that you would surely evaporate upon watching the torturous scorn of misguided and hateful actions spreading toward you and your loved one. What was the "secret" language to unlocking the dawning light? The language was merely opening the door to the thought of the actual existence of the dawn, just as you would open the door to the suffering, in which you would have chosen to see only hate. Rather, your decision was to take the perception that equilibrium would be restored with the Self-compassion of the one suffering in the insanity of hate.

Next, that I in the sky directs you to the complexion of what it was that engulfed you when you celebrated the order of humility and goodness in the face of the opportunity to dominate the actions of your sister. As well, you crafted the episode in which you were relocated into Your immensity via your only purpose being to master a task so that you might be privileged to watch as your brother enjoyed your love by receiving your service. You remember the material victory that was forsaken as a footnote and recall it only because it was the conduit to this chance you had to impart love. There was also the material goal you gained exclusively to benefit a deserving fledgling with intentions to Love thy Self and others.

These are the cases in which you achieved lofty positions and dispersed parts of Your unseen bodies into the fabrics We evermore dream to dwell. Let these reviving occasions incite you on your current way, that is, on the path to gaining a myriad of information that will empower your ability to create as We choose.

The link to Our welfare, which you assume is frayed, is more so when you are tattered from the sentiments of inadequacies after you did not manifest what you forget to notice is not essential to the "wealth" as it is defined outside of Earth's practical, fear-based standards. These are times when the desolations dim you because the intellect of the Light is not able to communicate to your mind your pretty posture on Terra, which is to roam in wonder with the harmonization of Self-Love as the searchlight, no matter the plight that society may tell you to recognize about your life. Love's score is there for you to grab from the forefront of your reactive mind when you are stunned by misconceptions into grasping like a child. Its mighty competence disentangles you from any picking, gnat-like annoyance that collaborates to dissuade you from recreating with the corrective mind. “Nothing is broken that can’t be fixed” was especially worded for you, since it is you who are destined to be officiating the conclusion of all you care to manifest.

When you execute your most admirable concentration with intent to favor love of Self or others, you abound within the breathtaking whirls of a Vitality with no apex as to the restorative information it can offer for your erudition. And so, as you:

- Dig that ditch to release darkness wherever situated
- Build the edifice to incite humanity’s grandeur and your own
- Lay the bricks to augment the spirit
- Solve the mysteries of universal logics for betterment of your brothers and sisters
- Plow the field to produce sustenance for all
- Commit to restore the health of humanity
- Add the numbers to organize lives
- Plot the way out of the box where you or your brother found yourself cornered within or the mud puddle you may have fallen into
- Care for those of frail mind, body, or spirit to aid them, and to learn about You
- Construct a phrase that will deliver to a brother a word that will engender the spirit of that “Love” you have since earned and learned,

then you have spoken with the omniscient All.

This is the same All where, when you are sufficiently practiced at the art of Self-love, you will find the transparency you seek in the meaning, intent, value, and direction in any given state of affairs you encounter.

52: THE NEVER-ENDING RECREATES YOU

You face Our seminal match-up with the relentless challenger to your Star's fluent shine. Taking into account the degree of your Light genius, little effort will be needed to ferret out the theme, which this time you received only as slight raps for the spotlight, being that you are mostly mindful of your predicament and have no desire to change and burry the facts you encounter. A vacuousness in your Star has developed from your courtesies, falling into the imperceptible hole of the temporary schemer's whims. These whims you count on to measure your choices. You have been persuaded that you are not sufficiently kind because you have no interest in the very attractive persuader's ambitions. The static within this empty chamber hails the theme. The freshly fortified directional device of your Star has informed You that this state of affairs will grant you merely disjointed fibers of Light to apply to your designs and to extend service to the grounding partners waiting for you to Lighten the trails.

Hence, comes your learned reaction, to preserve the primal shine of the Star's Light strands.

Expeditiously you recaptured it, sensing the robbery occurring to You upon allowing the ego to quench its thirst for approval by authorizing the clutches of a "very pretty and wily" one to enter with aggravations into Your abundant Lands. You easily employ your new idea: "Never more leave room inside for the authority of another to situate."

The finale to the plot was the unmitigated blow you delivered to relentless aggravations that collided with your Star. You saw no exigency in depreciating the deftness of your Star with the chaotic whims of an associate, partner or friend who relished their urgencies with no concern for your Fields, the same Fields where you bring about superior similes of You.

There is no value in validation from another. The one dictate for making my plans is the Light. It declares all the affectations that are draining the Self-determination of my Star.

The Entities that move forth with your paces gushed in a settling calm as you commanded your homecoming with Me, praising your less encumbered position here in 3D. Your adjusted judgments as to what is "pretty" now include being on the prized gateway Terra offers for you to bestow on your brethren everywhere—and for the Self—the product of empowering thoughts, words and actions resultant from actualizing your Light intelligence.

Excitedly thanking the grounding Earth for providing the way for you to hand out these riches is a lily embossed on your heart's river. The habitation of this passion will go on, commemorating that Your intact being carries an extra joy to offer—that is, absent your inventiveness being exhausted by appeasing your brother or sister.

Welcome home once more. The coalitions docking you to Earth were mystified that your Star, which was pledged to light their world, was less luminous than it is on this grateful day.

PART IX: WHO AM I?

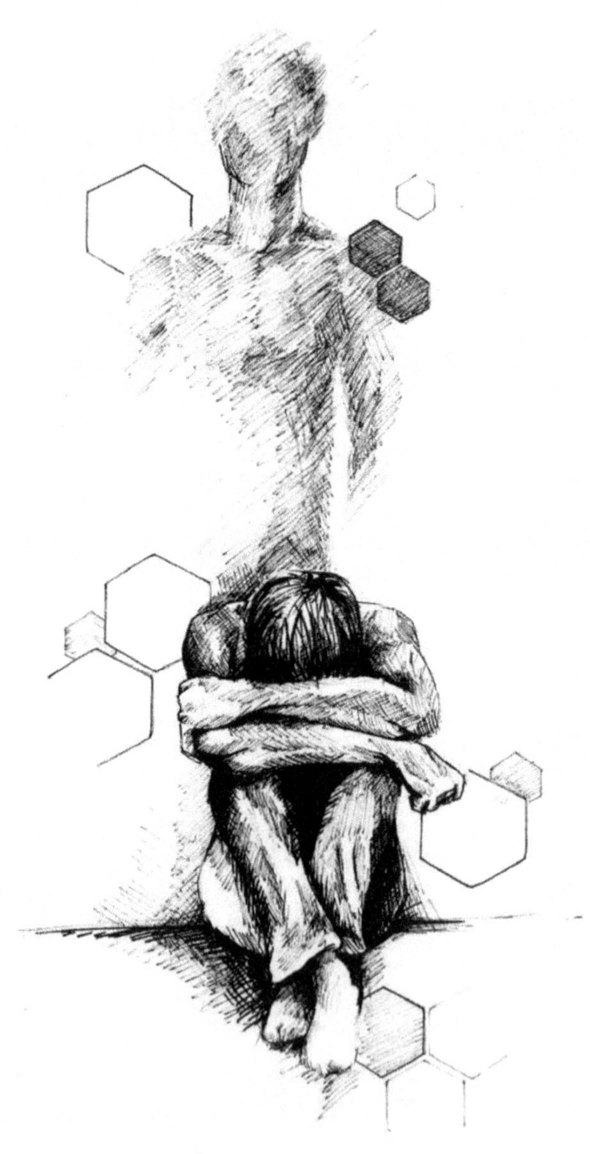

53: WHO AM I?

Who am I? A strand from a Star or the Central Sun, a soul, an alien, a multidimensional Being, a wanderer who came back to Earth to emit Light for the process of creation while I relay information to the Creator of Light? A messenger? A piece of the Creator?

All of that you are. You were born to realize the rarest of your Core that you can support by displaying it within the hybrids of Earth's ideological energy textures.

A researcher who spins prototypical Love-gold, exploited by expressions of life far and wide.

These are no analogies, rather situations depicting some of your many expeditions concerned with making contact with Your aggregate, whose outposts stretch well beyond this human physicality. You are your soul's representative on Earth, sent to advise the Celestials like Me.

54: YOU ARE YOUR INTENTIONS

When I cease with the wanting, the having, the cravings, and with feeling bad or good and instead only be, there is a signaling of cryptic scatterings of intelligence well above any of my prior deliberations. Practicing the use of these substructures I can't explain well. Identifying which actions of mine may stray from the brilliant savvy I apperceived from "just being," I unwittingly reduce my pace to test the circumstances which may or may not press me forward. I step aside from the ingenious signals in order to prove the result of my hypothesis, that when blindly treading into my curiosity I will suffer no digression. There is my misstep and where I often put off a maturity I expected, although I do not necessarily suffer a digression. I do discover why I felt it to be a "sideways" step. It was the indiscriminate intent with which I approached the step that caused the troubling pivot. Sceneries were revised, and I wound up face-to-face with the very realms in Self-love I always knew.

Your charts are multi-leveled. When you evade Our intended trail which We positioned straight so as to move you into fortunate circumstances you can rediscover the fluctuating templates that charge you. Find your depth perception through scrutinizing the intent with which your actions are delivered. Go forward with the assurance that your impetus is not of Earth's magically colored frequencies with their warm and sweet voices grasping for convenient pleasures and conquests without consequence to Our future. This point of reference is to be your power terminal when switching to the stations holding you afloat.

How many breaks along the way?

Broken are words of mankind that have no meaning to the universal You. Nothing of unconditional status in Being is qualified to be broken. Especially as to your current case where what has crumbled is your mental expectations of collecting a gain out of actions you claim to be your virtuous benevolence. Rectify the misinterpretation you have made of your actions. Prospecting to receive when you give your deeds partially to lighten your sister's burden is not your virtue but its contradiction when you are not clear in your approach. And your wish to secure an "earning" of any sort, or even an affectionate interchange, is part of your contradiction. Here, the only matter broken is your concept that your intentions were a generosity without attachments and your pride in being rejected after you have "given." These musings in righteous "giving" are meaningless without self-transparent gestures where you receive each human being with their perceived defects as an equal Soul in flight to the Light, no matter their part in the voyage, and no matter if you deem they bring only havoc and no profit for you.

Garnering this Love in action is the equivalent to an electrical vibration which maintains an all-encompassing acumen to rebuild the stretches it traverses. Universal Beings of Light are set nearby. THEIR attributes are Bands of omniscient and omnipresent illumination, a medicine of sorts used by the Troops who work for the placement of this Cure in every part of both the obvious and undeveloped structures of existence.

The beat of All that Is moves you to migrate with these universal Bands and inflate Them with Your unaffected loving kindness. Catching the tempo, an inflexible sternness in your Heart moderates, and modest fissures in your currents of Light are remedied as you replace your perspective that there was a "betrayer." In this case, it is you who have forsaken Our well-defined purpose to serve your sister with no forecast of a return to you. Draw the contrast. After all, you were not bartering in the rooms of the material masters, but ostensibly just offering a helping hand.

As you surmise, knowing that You cannot be "broken" simplifies the path toward you noticing the error in your thinking.

55: COMPROMISES OF YOU AND YOU

What of the universal negotiations which vie to take a piece of me? Am I a pawn in an organization outside of my comprehension in the here and now, where the I in the sky concurred in some way to contribute a bit of "Me" to the netherworld furies, fighting battles for their own devices? Am I in bondage to accumulating a stock of sublime usefulness from my virtuous Earth exercises in which other Energy beings are enriched with no worth to me?

Your original Extract, being without need of fleshly ingredients to be, is subject to no sacrifice. Universal, planetary, and human service to the "Love of All and You" is where your earthly, but detachable strings are linked to your Star. To differentiate, those pacts which were derived from innocent and altruistic ambitions from another day are cords ready at your wish and command to dissipate. That is, for instance, archaic pacts of poverty or many other vows which do not belong to You—disavow them. Check all thought structures you have patterned to live by which may waylay you from plenty. Actions and conscious and unconscious beliefs repelling the receipt of joy, love, and material sustenance should be set for extinction. Their kind, sensed as abrupt and tolling sounds laced with fear in receiving certain joys of being human—dislodge them without remorse each time they bubble with grief. Absolve yourself from all transgressions of your abuse in using abundance from any historical circumstance of any day and age.

All adherents to you that cramp your surroundings will in the end be your decision to throw into the avocations of Self-compassion for their reformation.

What is earned is received by the agent producing it, regardless of whether other entities are enhanced. In the transactions with You and the unknown "others," no deal that is invisible to You will abate your right to freely choose what you create and receive; that is, within the terms We set. These details have Your consent.

When you say "Your," is that the part of me that doesn't consciously know? This is fantastically absurd!

Existences from other stations in time and frequency cannot interfere with or adulterate Your love expression, nor can they weaken the dominance of the foremost Light Beings sitting closest to the origination of All, the Light of Creation. The Shield of these Beings' unconditional Love surrounding Earth's dominion is impenetrable. This is the covenant for those aligned with the Source of this Shield, that complimenting this Source will give you its protection from being trapped in "unseen deals" you may find unfavorable. The more common and contemporary Masters who infused part of their essence into vehicles humanity called the Buddha, Krishna, Muhammad, Abraham, Moses, or the Christ—whatever name you chose that inspires you to beckon the often-elusive Light of Love in your heart—are a portion of this buffer of refuge should you chose. As to the Christ, an Avatar some say, the force of his Being is part of Earth's insulate of Unconditional Love, a commodity known to All that Is. The remarks of the Christ about the meaning of the All sometimes cause a tearing. Out of misguided "Love" his supporters feel the need to draw comparisons and conclude that his essence was the most recent peak infusion of the Light of Creation into incarnate Earth form. Despite the accuracy or inaccuracy this assessment, the Christ's Being knows no need of equating its Essence as greater or less. If you are appropriately situated within the Light's presence to be capable of clearly absorbing its intelligence you will receive a transmission conveying the mental, emotional and energetic illustration that the Christ's presence is the Love within the All of the One. The Light is the place from which the I in the sky speaks. Regardless of the name of this insulating Energy of unbounded comprehension and presence, instilled with especially stalwart but compassionate truths, it is this all-powerful force which rules in spheres of 3D Terra. To state any of these Entities' composition is to describe all of Us. Moreover, to fathom this breed of Light's subsistence, or even the settings within which it abides, is one of the riches for your exploration and is peerless in all the galaxies. The universal law that trumps all others comes from these Entities' direction: the utilitarian energy of an unconstrained Love you don't fully conceive. These Masters are versed not just in beauty and love as you currently apprehend it. The forte of their Light essence in maneuvering throughout the ways of the envisioned and unforeseen durations of space and time is held in wonder throughout Collective Creation.

Has a Being outside of Us and the Light, to which We belong, okayed a concession to segments of You that are rightful to your personal and earthly fulfillment? No. The wanderer who is You has allocated all of You to the unified Us, not surrendering any shred. Such a logic fits precisely the Conventions guiding this manifestation of insulating Light of Earth: no dissipation, only escalation.

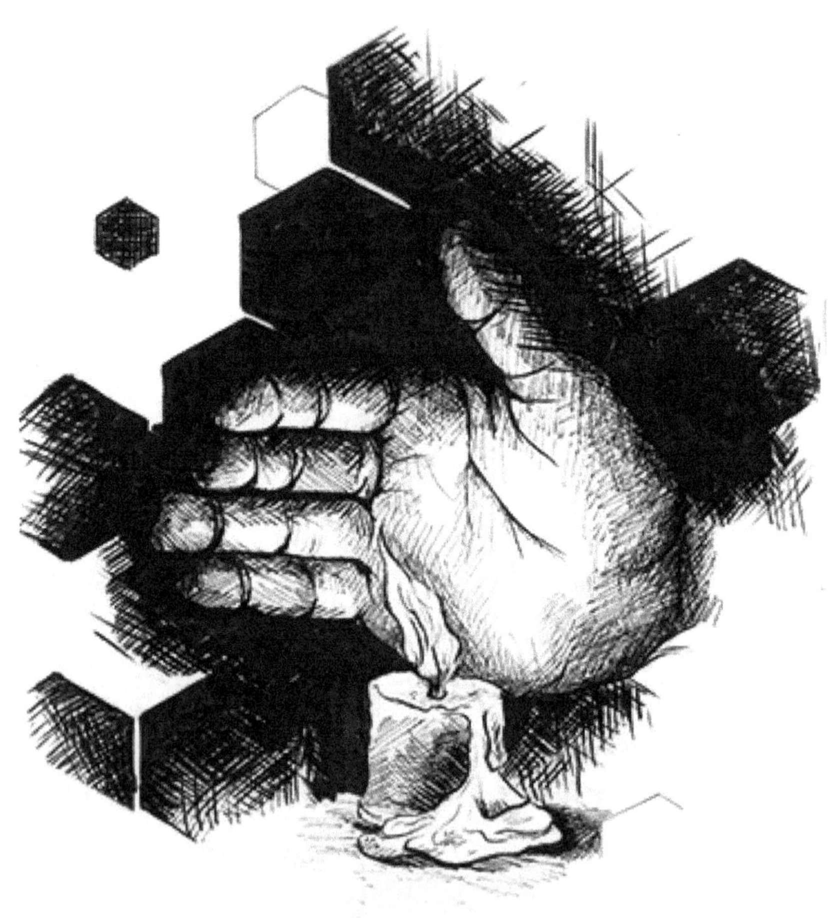

56: RATIONALES IN BREADTH

This ill-defined shape of Mine to which the I in the sky refers seems to fluctuate as I survey the way "upward."

Arriving at a true-to-form portrait of the majesty of a mountain all at once, as opposed to sighting it one chunk at a time, ordinarily the most pleasurable, is made more probable through the systematic purging that the I in the sky has I carved out for Us.

The remembrance of my distinctiveness within the collectives of creation is spread over too many planes, valleys, peaks, gusts of emotion, thought creations, gases, swales of water, and muck of muck that I can't translate it all together. I direct my target to take in the portions piece by piece. Higher peaks, lower peaks, deeper rises, small cliffs, airy and steep inclines, smooth foliage, pristine forests, translucent waters, and muck of muck. The Light shines on and through all variously, and each region hints of a change the more I attempt to see any spot as a part of the whole. Comprehension of the totality and how each chunk singularly ties into the entirety to make it as magnificent as its attributes are not mine. Too ancient a ground for my eyes? Me outside of sensory ideations, I can at times experience somewhat of a nascent filament unbothered by demarcations of physical space and linear time.

You galvanize the quizzical mind by your earnestness to hear the truth of Our constitution widening outward, solely so you may transfer your Grace into the All while in 3D. The characteristics comprising Our relations with Light matter turn with each of Your thoughts and actions, and with this, the truth of Your composition changes. Your inquisitiveness combined with an ardent aspiration to glimpse the ways to Self-love call the outer Beings of and with You. It is this Collection that announces from your Nucleus the peaks of its typography.

Here is a query for your use when you conjure the argument of you being a small and ineffectual being who is battered by the currents of chance:

If the never-ending or beginning Creator of Light initiates upgrades in the All of life's expressions with its delivery of pulsations of unqualified Love into the journey of everyone who pursues the way to "love thy Self and others," then do Your actions of imbuing in your thoughts and behavior unqualified Love for the cause of Self-prosperity, outer energies, or personages you happen upon have equal repercussion?

Same matter in, same matter out solves the riddle. This phase of yours in mortality, and that of all humanity on the Earth, is inestimable for the reason that You in fragile matter, with the determination of a Titan and a stately citizen, impact the progression of the universes. You are not a drop in any bucket to become an innocuous part of the whole, but an unending and perplexing marvel that is part of the Whole, gaining more dynamism with every practice of stain removal.

While You are partially staged in this physicality, you function as an amplifier of Us into the uninvestigated spectrums with rare acts in Love.

57: FOLLOWING STARS OF HIGHEST YIELD

Why wade in Earth's murky elements when there are pinnacles of bliss elsewhere? I could have a less cumbersome body and be experimenting in immensity within an orbit not vulnerable to Earth's whimsical sleeping pills. Why doesn't the I in the sky contemplate a soft cloud for Us to relax upon rather than send me to this orb and follow me around?

By and by, earthy fatigue permeates your attitude. You have taken your leisure upon many of these territories without this garment of flesh and have been disinterested upon first contact with the appearance of the surface. The Earth not being the initial place of manifestation from the Light of Our Creation, the soft vapors marked the beginning of your separation from the Creator of Light. You designated these clouds as un-redeeming. Then, there were the other more dense frames you carried in particular spheres in which you reached your upper plateaus. WE have come to accept that inhabitance on this third-dimensional orb is a singular prerogative. It is so, but not because it offers sensations meant for circumspect amusement that are inimitable elsewhere. It is Our choice because it provides you with rigorous exercises that enlarge your Source energy while you are physically embodied. With this coalition, you were meant to be dared into remote lands you had never identified and there live a prototypical model of You.

It is on Terra that you encounter misconceptions as to the Self with a level of density, coerciveness, and attractiveness in the warm and fuzzies which carry the potential to bring incapacitating doubts upon you by causing you to question the adequacy of your elemental composition. However, this is also where you have the option to manifest the most pristine expression of the Creator of Light's truth into an evolution for the All.

In other-matter frequency, We planned with excitement to be subject to this Earth stage, which is the very dominion in which to spawn these types of progressive revisions to Us, even while knowing the sensations can imprison you in the depths of insatiability, despair, and subversions of your divine will. You had a voracious appetite to enter into these provocations and transfigure them. Rekindle Your explanation for chasing these disguised invitations at a time when their propriety and Your exact caliber were correctly known. Your weariness was not anticipated during the stage in which We outlined Our strategy. Then you saw only your qualifications to easily move through all valleys you set out to trek. In this here and Now you will lose the fatigue by welcoming the tools to your refinement, which is living on Terra with the malleable mix of the Graces as your defenders while you see through the eyes of a cleansed Star.

And should you be called to in the here and now, you agreed to show gallantry while in tender flesh. In your current land, which understands the loss of the delicate garment humanity wears, you promised to be fearless when implanting the rod made of your backbone to champion the cause of the powerless from abuse of power. You willingly agreed to take all chances possible to convey examples of the destruction that can be born from the desire to acquire exclusively for the fictional self's interests without thought to how the road to the possession may affect your brother or sister. You accepted with zeal the task of thwarting actions that are spun from hate which dominate or endanger a humble brother or sister. You welcomed the role of being the warrior soul who forgoes these destructions that lend the need for the hero. You swore against the use of the hostilities of the Earth plane and accepted that you would not direct them against those who oppose your ego's definitions of appropriate human traits.

Then there was the valiant pact you accomplished when you, surrounded in the dim vapors of leisure, initiated the blast out of these gases trapping you so powerfully that you had no regard as to who in your charge was slighted by these idle relaxations.

Your behavior during your entire stint on this go around on Terra proves that you have sided with the doctrine of opposing, with your loving presence and active will, all ties with the ravages of hate and intolerance that some permit to characterize humanity. The yield gathered by the All from this code you lived courageously will be told as time unfolds for you here on the Earth plane. The I in the sky will give you a clue as to the size of such a feat: the Being of your cleansed Star can abolish every division bringing humanities' anguish by meshing your steadfast resolve to "Self-Love" coordinate with the opening in your Heart-mind, thus enabling the Star's pulsations to direct you to Its highest yields.

Never will the repetition of these words be wasted: MY composition—a lofty and malleable one that bends and does not tear and is impervious to gashes or lacerations—has no access to these unnerving liaisons with whom you sought to take a trek through Terra. That is why the Me here in the less weighty invades your every thought. You hold the distinction of intimacy with the mighty leap you secure when You trust the armor of Love's fortress during uncertain crises similar to those in which you restrained others who recklessly prowled for pragmatic terrestrial gain. These are the same ones who have authority over vast material resources and who are versed in the ways of bringing misery and limited days to the non-compliant. It was your effort that opened their eyes, thus preventing the blind exaction of hurt from occurring to a few fellow humans who held no posture of being harmed.

You must be speaking of the wrong person. Me, this one who has been banging the same concrete wall, I am the master of nothing more than a few whimsicals.

Reminder: you often break through the concrete. Being too harsh on yourself is a tightness. Free it. It is the same You in the Now whose yesteryears prove you sojourned the valleys and mountains of previous description. The time has arrived to entertain the fact that these are your historical deeds, a postulation you must understand is no longer too fantastical considering that the boundary between Our Selves has been lessened.

The crusading skills I picked up evade me, as do my present aspirations.

Because these annals of your stories elude your memory does not mean the perceptible diagram of the accomplishment secured is not there for you to use as a reference for future encounters. And not only from Earth. Your performances, particularly on Terra, remain exclusive to you and to all of those scholars incarnated on her beloved surface. They are unattainable elsewhere in the All, which mixes spaces, times, and frequencies. As you have intuited, Terra's spectrum of frequencies is the most vast in the All of energetic manifestation.

Choosing where you were going to manifest was prudently studied when you had an exact awareness of the potentials of Our expressive resources held within Our universal Essence. While this Essence has never quit thumping in your heart, you have not come to know it as a conscious "reality" in any Now you have lived on Earth.

Naturally, if you consider the repercussions of your noble service to the Light only by the posture your physical eyes exhibit as your creations, then of course the grandeur of all else You have instituted and can institute, which is impressive by cosmic standards, is overlooked.

WE are sworn to never judge from a mindset of the petty or the small, but to have as our reference point Stars of Our highest yield.

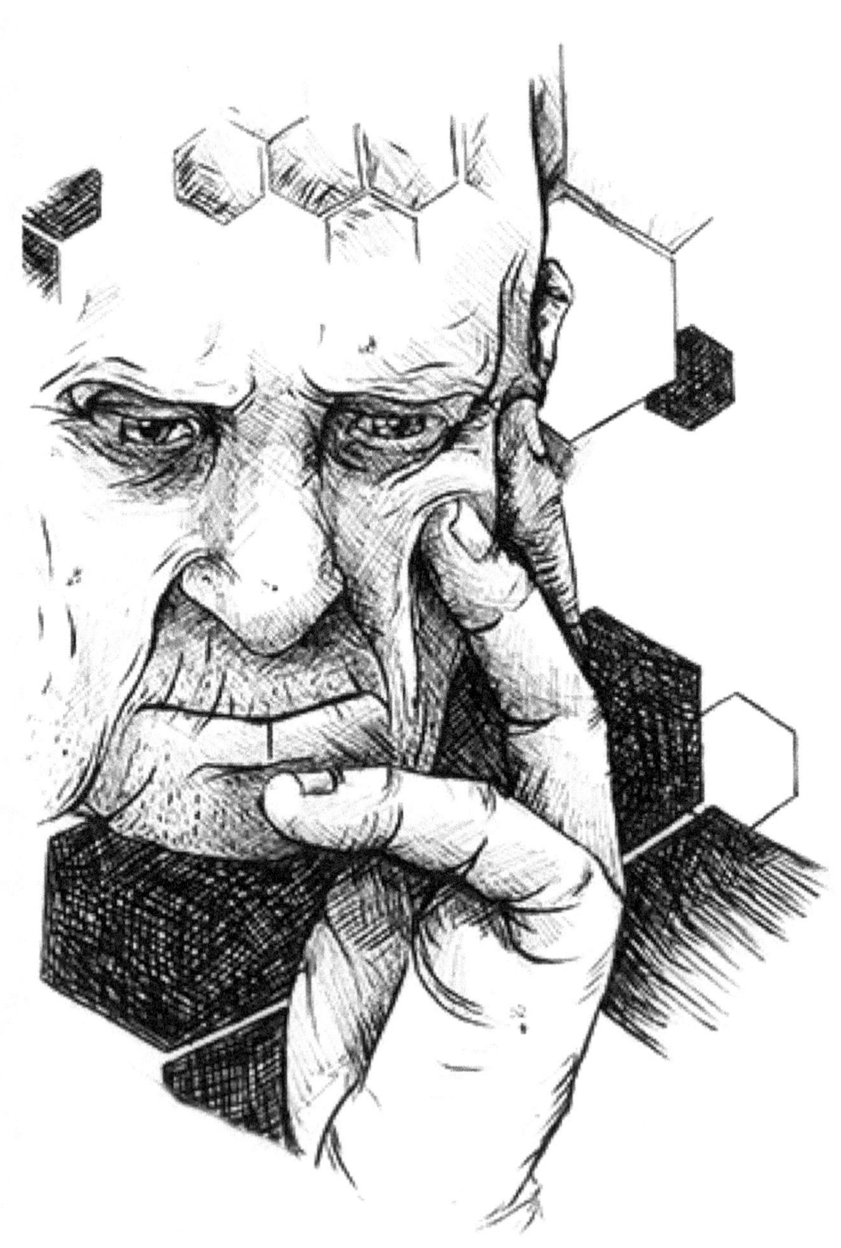

58: QUELL THE TREMBLING

You fell prey to the dim frauds when they persuaded you to join them as they mimicked sentiments of the "pristine" shores of your curiosity and then could not deliver the shore you sought. Another ill-conceived intention or foggy face? You shudder. To calm yourself, you need to be convinced that you have left behind all variants of you that indiscriminately acquiesced to the illusionists guarding your hole. Then you need be quieted by the reality of your uplifted stance. These enchanters are no longer the sentinels to your cavern. They are hunters of the elusive you.

Me, I am not smart enough to stop my sweep into useless use.

What is useless is relative to where you have set your sights. What you refer to as earthy "instincts" have earthly reactions and have a purpose for these earthly components surviving as forces apart from your Star. Your relaxation with the lazy natures brings shivering that is derived from subjective impulses of some ambiguous "casualty" with which you punish yourself. It is unbearable for you to even briefly reflect that you may have crossed the line you laid to prevent from entering an unsafe haven. And so, you panic from the possibility of the tunnel backwards containing a crevasse that will swallow You. The relief to your scare is that there is no stopping you from scaling Our cliffs due to this latest circuitous routing of your time. Eliminate the pain from your fear. In fact, that route has potential for advantage if the I in the sky can be heard.

Instituting easily accessible corridors for the I in the sky's thoughts is becoming a reliable custom of yours.

Eradicate the trappings of self-denunciation by easing yourself through it with a "Self-tolerance" found in the belief that You can undergo no damage, although you can be better informed. Once you have taken away the fault, get a fix on the productiveness in this stumble. What features are you counting in the lazy natures which are the source of the trembling? That you are them? That is a destructive inaccuracy. They are faceless imposters that pose as part of the human species by pretending to be your natural likeness. It is easy to confuse them with something they are not, which is part of Your texture in human form. This variety of Earth matter is akin to silhouettes in misty warmth, mimicking Mother Earth's sympathetic grandeur. Though, unlike Mother Earth, they do not have the Light as a reference point as they whittle their substance into thought conjectures and posture themselves succinctly for your acceptance. The misty warmths throw seemingly authentic flares of what is ostensibly organic matter in random sensuality, hunger, unquenchable thirst for more of what you hunger for, thought postulations confusing you as to your nature, and their favorite, the attraction found in mental laziness, all posed for you to welcome them as part of your Being. They tell you that you have unbreakable unity with them. Yet, they are intruders into your Light bodies, especially the emotional body. Because you are not circumspect in your thoughts, you don't see that they are endemic to the atmosphere of Earth, but not of Earth's essence. Likewise, they are not of Your or Our essence, but merely temporary visitors to your shell to whom you frequently have permitted entrance. If this separation is not made, it is an easy mistake to assume that when you capitulate to their posturing, you feed You. That is where you can be lost in turmoil unless, when you taste their flavors, you do so in carefully measured steps by remembering that their glittery beams are distinct from your Star's Light. And this you may do unless you invite them in as integral to You. Nor are they part of your biological, 3D anatomy, although they frequently do swirl within your emotional bodies at your behest.

You picked it up, My apt Earth partner. The word *lazy* is the theme, the rhythm, and the sign. The spin of what is striking in that word tells you that you are slighting something when you are *lazy*. What you deny when you opt for excessive entertaining with Earth's endemic creatures can be access to more extensive sensibilities in which you are adaptable to a variety of heightened faculties you never postulated. Be attentive to Your universal positioning when the posturings knock. Upon the arrival of the Earth plane's bullets, which carry the capacity to restrict the functioning of your emotional body, there is a decision to be made between Grandeur and the misty clouds.

Come nearer, my Earth agent, and let me have the privilege of imparting to you my words. Yes, it is that which I speak of instantly and it is meant to enfold you with Love.

With your modern orientation you follow My language with fierce concentration. The sureness of your days to come, your many ambitious expectations depicting You as a dependable and unique prodigy for whichever output We chose to sow, and with the Star lighting your sometimes incomprehensible but wondrous field while transmitting in mental channels that subdue alarms of any proposal of your smallness—there emerges your mighty Field.

PART X: THE BLINDNESS IN BETWEEN

59: ANGER

Yes, I am happy to be hooked here in the home of the furies, dominated by the physical where I trust only that which I can touch with my conditionally existing hands and smell with my conditionally smelling nose and taste with my temporary senses!

Revisiting muck. The eyes of the I in the sky are splattered with the soot of your outrage in distrust, speculations of betrayal, and daggers thrown with no concern for You. Causal body soil swells. While you are integrating into your cellular and Ethereal bodies and standard thoughts a more effortless alternative than purely 3D sensory operations, you do have the intention to clean yourself up. Notwithstanding, the correct foresight deserts you at this fork in your road. Your everyday behavior has not seen the revitalized properties you fancy as a consistent state. You walk now in two very different worlds and see the dichotomy between them. Your chaotic inner thrashing divides you from Me, the Me who you have surmised knows not the discord you confront. The Me in the calm space of perfection, without the awkward and burdensome difficulties you flail within, has only omnipotent solutions that radiate peace and Love. You resent advice from this haven. You don't believe there to be any chord of sincere appreciation from Me for your situation amongst the confusions.

Yes, if discernment were an effortless skill to acquire the word confusion would have no use.

It is the correct proposition: which of the competing influences will you choose out of confusion?

That Me in Lighter weight sees opportunity in what you face, just as some time ago You swore to enthusiastically seize the possibilities to Our liberation held within the destinations We plotted for you, including wandering on Terra's universally alluring green orb where her atmosphere would be filled with the throbbing sensations of anger and disorientation. The only different condition now that you have arrived on Terra is that you are actualizing the experience that was the subject of Our plotting session without having the benefit of the translucent acquaintance you had with the omnipotence of the Graces, as you did when We were scheming your adventures. Then, you were certain that the Graces were your unfailing champions during the thickest of forays. Just for an instant, can you reject the defeating energies and contemplate this other fine time when your size was known? Riveting anticipation was your reaction when you, in Lighter embodiment, reviewed what were to be your 3D studies you now meet.

You have nothing to prove, my respected Earth copy. The Light synthesis formerly accrued by you is vested for your exercises to come. The process of integration We seek is certain.

While wedged amidst this fiction of you as having a small status, search for the jovial quirks of the Light's charms that is to be found in the awkward stance you sense. Being that your modern approach to any abstract branding of your circumstances, or those of others, employs Light intellect to make the assessment then try the term the "beautifully comical" to Judge your predicament. This imaginative illustration will allay the suspicious hostility you assume is a dichotomy in your life.

More to the truth, I live the "profoundly absurd."

Shout while you believe in it, if you like. Someday, it will not seem absurd, but instead a logical consequence of your journey. Otherwise, you will reap scarcity and cozy up to the disquieting annoyances.

Disquieting? Disabling is what they have been.

The bitterness is understandable while the fortune you have engineered has not entirely fused into your bodies. Superficial sores on your physical body are chips in the chest of the vile-spirited angers. For an encore, these jolts are quickly returned to you, like energetic boomerangs. I come prepared to eradicate my Earth ambassador from the disembodied spirits of madness that are pummeling you into scorning and blaming. These will not be enough to reposition you away from the many debuts of which you are deserving, but which you have not definitively envisioned.

I am doused and ambushed everywhere I look. Powerful barricades push against me. Where are the Allied contingents, the Partners in competence the I in the sky has endorsed!

You have barred Their involvement by right of your decision. Rage combats the Troops you extol.

If They are willing to abandon me while I am ambushed, They are not worthy colleagues.

THEY are companions that mesh with you in your performances—if you discard your compromising rage. THEIR tender speech praises your breath on Terra and your opportunity to enact countermeasures to any imbalance.

Exactly. The heart softens just now, turning with the attractiveness you regard in being exposed to Earth's surface elements, which you have just scorned. The I in the sky is inspirited by your shift into the Now, where you arrive at gratefulness' calming status after having opened to see Our total meaning to the All while looking through the senses of a human on this ceremonial Earth. You enfold yourself with the alluring thought that it is this Earth which has given you the means by which you can create inimitable manifestations of You.

60: CONTINGENT AFFILIATES AND BOUNDARIES DISSOLVE

OUR inevitable reunion. Your grids are refreshed from what We last noted. You took a jaunt with stubborn righteousness. When "injustice" in your interactions with your brothers and sisters was your ordeal, when wounded with rage from "unfairness", organizing a curing strategy to recover in a barbed-edged course deposited you just there, in the barbs. Your attempt to remove the "wrongs" was filled with "fairness" flares, which kept Me inert. When infuriated from "offenses," cutting ties between Us is the most elemental terrestrial fix.

Was it moments ago or years ago? From what I see, much has come and gone. The I in the sky narrowly regards time changing from reconfigured Light patterns in your surroundings. There are no longer outlines of "injustice" to devote your fiery crusade. Your schooling has been received, that rage at inequity is ineffectual when used to try to tip the scales of "justice." This is especially the case when you have not considered the many components of "justice." How could you understand the full scope of this concept of "justice" when your vision comes only through a small channel? Certainly, animosity will not open a wider angle.

This impairing resentment you generated from what you saw as an "injustice to you" fastened you and Our Star to the weight of denouncing the subject of your fury, the purpose and origin of which you never fully appreciated.

The feedback from the Ethereal is mobilization of the backup teams. They will lend you a hand so as to aid the cause of your recently constituted logistics, absent the fiery scars.

Your more acutely aligned and further reaching mind permits the I in the sky to succinctly reproduce Our collective direction here. You veered from the brandings of "injustice" and improvised, theorizing that the embroilments were at least partly fashioned by Us. That is, even another segment of Us—not you individually—committing acts that contradict Love's expression in the corporeal, which you don't succinctly recall. Your stately consciousness took on the role of importing into your current appearance on Terra the experience of what would appear to you as an "injustice" so that you could summon through your earthly eyes this hurt inside of a part of Us that called for a special conciliation with the truth of Our involvement in the "injustice." This was to be a restoration to equilibrium of certain dissonant energies affecting what you now know as the broader Us.

There is another part of Us?

There are many for whom we commit Our Valor.

That critical peek you dared to welcome exposed a part of the collective Us having similar behavior as your contemporary "nemesis." You ease into the possibility that your brother's playing field was once skewed when he was delivered a less than "fair" interpretation of facts at a moment when he was making decisions critical to his Earth journey. The healing tonic, which you have begun to practice well, is to withdraw from the torment with no animosity or regret, an intact and fully empowered being, as always. You resigned the "need" to fight from the stance of "victimhood" by calling out and battling a corruption. Gone is the tarnish of claiming an "inequity" to yourself. It is pleasing to Me to watch you unload from You the feel of wrongdoing as you regain the upward movement with little loss in your stride, just as one might briskly discard a limb from the trail while trekking within the wilderness.

Assigning your indignations a small scale by not endorsing them with your denouncements minimizes the struggle you commit to animosity. And, this restructuring marks the return of your envoys, who blend with you into the refurbished blueprint of Our initial approach.

Meaning?

You steadily sustained a plateau of vibration that squared with preparedness for encountering more ground to surmount, at your side efficient honing devices of Light. Here your ingenuity bursts ahead of delimiting altitudes you once claimed as belonging to you.

61: CODES AND KEYS

You appear in the chamber with the shimmering crystal chandelier and disregard not only that the space is lit, but also the origin of the Light that permits you to walk without knocking into walls and also how it refracts into countless places in and outside of the room and through the windows to places unnoticed. This image is similar to how you encounter your waking moments when you forget that, as you are living in flesh, there are appreciable keys, codes, and symbols for debuting to you other parts of Our summit. The I in the sky calls them codes because the only measure that will reveal the information within the setting before you is your investigation into it. It is not meaningless scenery. Disincarnated souls and otherwise who abide within the sight of the Light prod you to ingest the instruction embodied within the figurative announcements that are to be your retreat out of every stupor. Inflections in words, symbolic engravings in atypical movement, hard and fast obstruction of practicalities, the receipt of material to share, hellos and goodbyes, vistas into empty and full rooms and gates to exit from—along with any other means to keep you in conforming sequence to your Star, including pain—can be platforms from which to leap from one to the next.

Moreover, within the protocols of Terra's free-will zone, the Light workers abide by a convention that strives to deprive Us of every affair that is inclined to negate your accessibility to Our Light Archives We have stockpiled for maximal performance. This is done with the consent of Me, your best Self. The upsurge of crystalline Light into your 3D bodies repels any thought form that attracts your moves away from the way to strengthen your visibility. With enough stubbornness, you can override even the crystalline transmissions directed to you by Me and the legions of Light. Although, situations that have the wherewithal to scatter your spotlight away from Our mark have rhyme and reason. Certain hurdles to what you solicit are set with gestures of caution, which appear as the hurdle's mix of challenges, or pain.

What is the clue behind your anxious gushes during these trials of yours that end with a pronounced alarm of the indignation of "defeat"?

Predictably, we reappear for the recurring topic of your careless grasping with delusions of "need," but truthfully, they are nothing less than tantrums of "want", to again persuade you toward the possibility of an educational cadence in the "deprivation," which you scream exists as deterrents to your plans.

You burn the courage of your Star when you seek to depict the completely exposed composition of a sadistic seduction that is coupled to your waves of emotion of "want." Yes, you have spotted the strenuous comment of threats to you—a "you" which you are not sure about—due to the denial of one of the utilitarian aspirations sanctioned by society. There, you notice that this "threat" carries you into further embroilments in nearsighted and muddled fixes of "you" due to desiring a sanctuary in the pragmatic.

Disband the myth within your storm embankments that see You as having any defect, lack or poverty that can imperil you. If not, you are suspended in the neurosis and muck of "wanting." Confined by this "deprivation," you grab randomly at any object to cure this state of affairs.

In other words, the next best thing to successfully ridding yourself of disruptive ideations of "want" is a tangible object as a resting spot for the lazy mind due to shortsighted fatigue. It is a temporary prop-up for the Earth self while We tirelessly search to expose your Earth eyes to your Star's provisions, having no notion of "want." This prop-up is usually a mud puddle for the Star.

Within the numbing insecurity of not having enough is My utterance of the pointer to your way out. It is as uncomplicated as accepting that it is no compromising defect of Yours when you are unable to attain the conquest you coveted within your lower comfort zone.

As you consider the alternative solutions to "want", the I in the sky sees you sitting upon the threshold of uncovering the pleasing mysteries of life that involve expressing the generosity of the Star's Heart, thus displacing all "want" to acquire externally.

It is reasonable that the inflection of Your perfect wholeness is as uncomplicated as the gift you have acquired of a wondrous smile that permits you to sincerely express you care when a gentle soul is in need of knowing they are loved. Or, in some way, you are working on accumulating this smile for reviving the spirit of hope in all who care to look. Rather than the smile, it could be any other mannerism, word, or phrase of gentle empathy you birthed from the bold recognition that the one you labeled "nemesis" suffers worse pains, and you forward this sentiment to the "enemy." Perhaps it is the promise to believe that the love in the relationship is the only aspect that is trustworthy of being sustained and refuse the attraction you have for material luxury that forcefully grips your partner in episodes of anger and stress. Perchance, the prospect for your enjoyment is of a physical nature, say, an edifice you were to build with safeguarding determination. Deliberate on the ditch you may dig with the stamina to diffuse obstructed channels in Yourself or the Earth. Can it be a place you were to visit so that others might gain your light in their "dense forest"? It is even plausible that you can foresee detecting a new procedure for stylizing matter that is to be established throughout the Earth's healing professions, or assisting or inspiring one to do so. Positively you see your generosity as your commitment to improve your relationship with the dignities of Our Affinities so as to guide your charges' growth by way of you making exemplar introductions to them of the Graces.

Picture, it: you having served another to attain social status because there was a neglect in times past. Monetary repayments for your part in money lost are common to finish a circle with a returning Earth associate. Could it be that what propels you to relaxing your mind is acquiring the art of generous patience toward another when you show compassion by silencing of your ego in the face of constant shots of fear and fury? You offer support and not acrimony. Can it be as rare as a goodbye with an intent and pronouncement of unconditional love that both you and the other are at peace in the farewell? The scenarios of kind generosity are as numerous as the traces of Light from your Star, which are inexhaustible.

Base all your intentions in the Graces, and you will meet no crippling fantasy of defect if future opportunity anticipated, which is heavy in your focus, is missed in the process. Within Our Heart of prosperity, you will know the grandest "code" or "key," living only what We admire, all your mental formulates tolerating no space for "want."

62: BLIND AMBITION

This all appeases my depths if I am looking from the limited angle of being in a tunnel. Nonetheless, the deeper examination is how far up the ladder are deals made that ensnare me? Does the unseen "Me" agree to these very convincing energies of "threat" and "want", apparently shepherding me to see great opportunity when I train with the Graces, primarily because the resulting energy I design from the engagement is a component to benefit a larger scheme? My feeling is that pacts are made between what I call universal separations of Affluence, where these differing forces of Affluence and influence are disparate and mutually exclusive—no unity, but opposition. Earthly subjects are recruited on teams for the adversaries' relevant purpose. What you tell me are my gracious thoughts and actions are for their ends. Are my "deprivations," temporary or otherwise, an outgrowth of these stellar accords?

My expeditious recasting of what I see as a hardship into Self-worth is a product that is traded!

Your Star is now well fertilized. Notwithstanding, evasions from Our work at hand abound. While on this topic, Your entire Nucleus, which is not situated here on Earth, acts as a component in this system of satisfying pacts with the universal influences you reference, yours being bound to the Light Affluence. YOU aspire to commit to a team that walks in an order unseen. Isn't it fantastic? You are an agency within an "orderliness" that obliges you to the task that bursts You into a Light metamorphosis far outside what your consciousness can consider.

Fantastic. And it is tempered with the flash that the law of free will similarly enable me to attract what I may see as brutality if my choices are not wielded with virtuous circumspection, and the word that the I in the sky gave to the barter He made. And worse, you speak of a cognizance I here on Terra presently don't have!

Not ever will it be a "brutality," but solely a discomfort that is suited to underline certain critical idea vestiges that are not in tandem with Light energy protocols concerning your development.

Shunning the site of the thunder that dispatches the avalanche of aches because you consider yourself enslaved within a system that ignores Earth's practical norms is a tantrum that does not register with any leverage to any authority of consequence.

Back to the codes and keys. Shift the turns of your Star with your intrepid heart. Intuit the message in the pain of the scare. Persist. Catch your part in spawning the fear with the help of that beam you can nearly see with your physical eyes as it permeates you in a way similar to an energetic vision. The radiance you catch between the zealous contours in panic is where you isolate the hidden truth of your slate, cleansed of unworthiness, incompetence, and want. It is within this instance that you will render yourself meritorious of all riches. And, where you will breed with Self-love which knows no "discomfort".

WE scribed this act in a restorative healing arts session prior to your latest embodiment. Back then, this scene We have finished was contingent upon the many brave steps you have already walked. And, it surpasses many of Our probable expectations. Give credit to this inventiveness We dispatched.

An "unreal" agony of your sacrifice or your victimhood streams from the grandest deception, that you encounter a paucity of magnitude, or free will.

You confirm the identity of the glare. It is your very own Star, showing you that there is no shortfall in You, nor any lack in any part of You that you need to compensate for by proceeding onward in actualizing your culture's sanctioned successes. Such societal victories are to be in the order of Our rankings.

Extend thanks to your flame of angst and rage, which you subdue with the Light's capital. It was with these emotions that you sourced and recovered part of Your presence outside of "wanting."

The Graces are the perfect tuning fork to put in place the illustrious pitch of Your concerto and strike another string of the shimmering You.

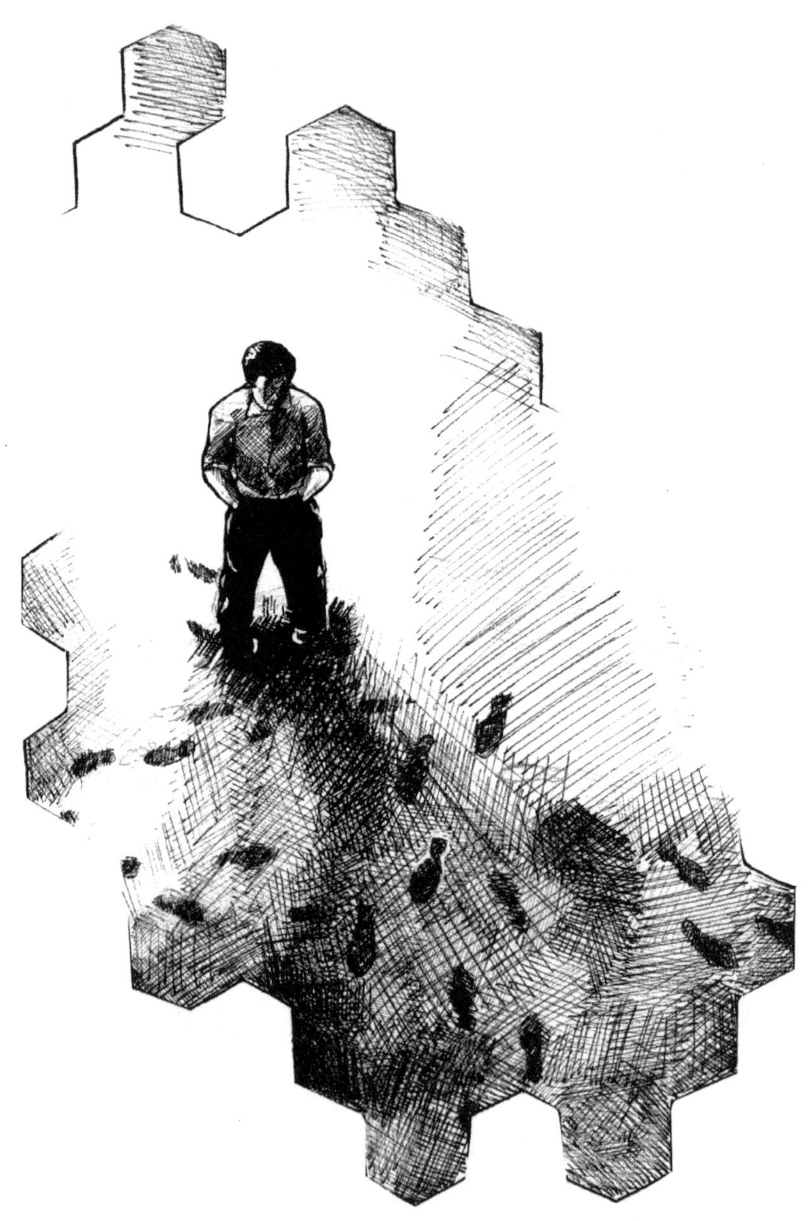

63: NEVER KNOWING

My every breath in this skin I missed the fact that the shrewd ones, those that shielded my discoveries of the potential available to me, were hovering close and within my forms. This effectually veiled my eyes from receiving the disseminations that lie on the other side of their barriers. My grave hazard? I would have been oblivious to even a shred of my autonomous Being that was not reliant upon the Earth's elements and survived simply as a sensually instinctual being.

No. Your deal with Yourself was that upon Your coming into the physically appreciable you would withstand jolts of the variety known in the netherworld so as to satisfy Our covenant of implementing an adequate wake-up call. Jolts of this severity were made necessary by Our election to abolish from your emotional bodies the shears of the gales of a serious sort and the chains naturally consequent to their causes—your and "Our collective" previous mindless deeds. WE knew these whirling energies would keep you heavily transfixed within their force field. Remember the freezing rain? Although at the same time, the outcome was foreseen due to the carefully computed promise that you could summon the degree of Light Capital to transmit a signal to be heard by components of Light that are receptive to the sorts of beacons you would emit, including your own Star within your own Earth Self. The transmission was received, and a life line of an ardor your contemplative brain has not discerned was sent.

Spotting the artifices as more than a myth was assured via the robe you wear, fabricated from Light-Love. You were to acknowledge, as you did, this adornment being held captive when its sound of triumphant wonderment hailed that particular function of your Heart that afforded you conscious reception of its salute. Such enunciation declared its hope to breathe within decorations designed with Self-love throughout Terra. A more lucid line of transmission it could not have been. Light correlation without fail makes its departure from even the cleverest of intricacies and attaches to its equivalent. It is gained in an instant, and not just from bringing it with you to Terra, as yours mostly was.

Gained Light Love is quantifiable? Increase in Light Love lends itself to measurement?

More powerful words than "is gained", the I in the sky suggests for you would be the words "brought in".

You are imbued with doubt that a calculation can be made. And, why should you not believe that math is a part of the world of Love's energy, just as finite calculations are to your material scientists? This potency does not dissipate, but transmutes all that allows its entry to a Lighter configuration. Amplitudes that you have taken in with Self-love occupy Your storehouse of Light acumen for your use upon your calling.

And, you guessed it: it is not adapted within by the desire to amass it. It is only prone to "assembling" by the most innocent intent to liberate you or your earthbound brothers and sisters from pain and its causes or to show to them the causes of happiness, or by materializing a prowess which lauds the Love of thy true Self.

PART XI: THE ETERNALLY, FURTHER CALLING

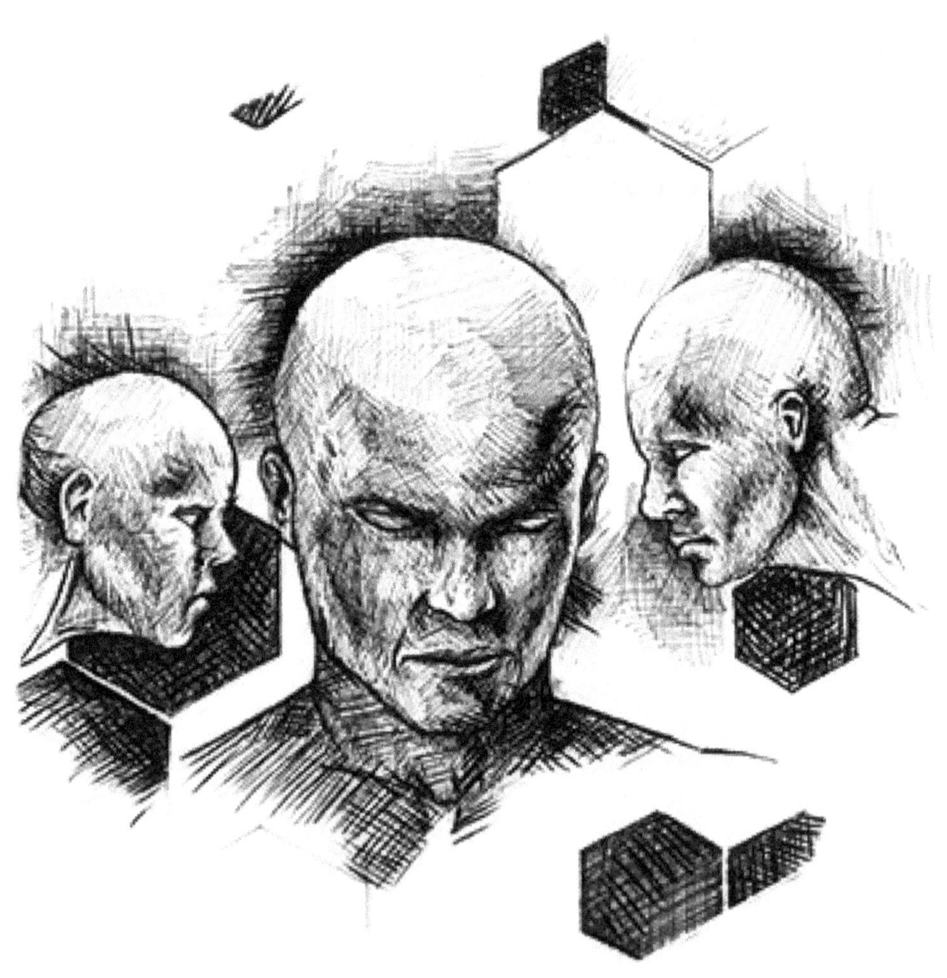

64: DECORATIONS IN CONTRAST

The next room to be probed, as you are aware, is the one We never deliberately planned for you to defiantly enter, or otherwise. But then again, look at what you have left behind and taken in its place. This room alludes to a lovely invite with its striking mental decorations throbbing as a mystifying parable in your learned Heart. This sensation seduces you toward testing your bravery so you may be further educated. It is, that these are the stunning sectors where your recently stepped-up Light brothers anticipate merging with you and Your prowess so as to make contact with the muted partitions that adjoin these ornaments.

Your declarations of this jubilant state you intend to sustain has prepared you to intake Light data to entrench within Your systems, so you may unravel further axioms that will assist your sojourns to come.

During this process of accomplishing my "initiatory arrangements in fresh conditions" I came to learn such captivating words of the I in the sky as a precursor to getting in touch with a uniquely nimble spirit, which I will need if I am to locate the meaning in these obtuse decorations, which initially sneaks in as a feasible approach to improved equilibrium. Then, afterwards, when I see the foundation of ideas I have accustomed my life around defy the existence of what has now evolved into the I in the sky's very taut suggestion, I am jolted into disarray. I notice what are potentially fairly uncomfortable truths in wading into this parable. It is no less than a mandate that I take a serious second look at what I have ordained as "truths" that organize my life. The consequence? Reordering my life, once over!

I am overwhelmed by the advancing disconnect between the current standards that prop up the foundations I use to organize my life and this seemingly credible revelation in the parable demanding that I consider its viability to shed cords of edicts I live, ones that keep me in density, or that keep me from "more."

And the I in the sky is disturbingly quiet!

What fairness is there in condemning innocuous acts as life-negating behavior. Does the I in the sky instruct me that my balance is negated and the order in the path to Me can be nullified by one, if not all, inoffensive styles? It is not obvious to me which— if not all— are the lines to my debilitation: adorning the body, the use of the body, the desirability of attributes of the body, ingestions into the body and the reasons for them. They are styles that have no reason to bother another. And speech or behavior that will call out the truth of an unjust or hateful intolerance should never offend the I in the sky or any other. My unyielding stance against random oppression and resolve to fight its spread must be a welcome quest to those higher Lines of Love that are pulling me upwards. Conscientious protest adds to productive discourse. Then there are the well-meant affections; whatever the class, they take nothing from anyone. They only add to the sentiments of caring and respecting, what are a form of Love. Then there are.........

Yours are not all of those.

What may be inoffensive "styles" for another are informative courses for you, just as inoffensive "styles" for you are informative courses for another. Compare your disposition to no one's. If you dare look, obvious before you are histories of yours that will take you to untenable conceptual contrivances that are bonded with your emotional bodies and divide You from optimal fitness. There is a Self-deception of fairly large proportions, which has the tag of being innocuous, assisting in forming the overall fractures in your Light-line transmissions. Be forewarned, this impending Self-disclosure is an incident in the thickest intermixture, a state of affairs you presently suppose would be unfair condemnation of Self and others if you were to change your opinion on the matter.

You hold steadfast to the position that this habituated opinion needs no inspection.

These dominant ideological quandaries of yours are foretold to be reintegrated as Lighter body "axioms," with no negative verdicts lingering. At a later date you will no longer place a directive upon yourself to misguide your mind so as to preserve uneducated opinions bearing labels of "justice" or "fairness." Your consciousness doesn't conceive the locus of these lesions. Upon these subjects, you have not given Me permission to engage you straightaway. You, being the final arbitrator of the "truth" you prefer to live has laid down layers of optimal philosophies written from a powerful sense of "justice" and "fair play," which are Our disunion. These molds in "purity" of judgment do not come off unless your centermost points are rocked. As the intervals of your life turn and you confront them all, the result will be the disabling of these Self-betrayals and again, seemingly, will come a shattering of your "identity."

In time, the bravery formed out of your desire for Self-actualization will be roused. And with this, the lamp will be hoisted on the reason for confusion in your rationales for "just" and "fair." The injustice you know as "judgmental ideas" must, from what I can see of the soundness of your energy layouts, eventually be noted by you as windows to Your universal truths, without connotations of right or wrong.

The beginning of the way to resolving the monumental perplexities you confront was marked by your cooperation in unshackling Your planes of affluence. This initiated a type of energetic tension within your bodies. It continues now as it pushes you to entertain the chance that all behavior and ideas must be assessed for their propensity to stain You, not another. WE accepted stresses to bear down upon and overpower the defenses you organized around these "justice" gates. Where these designations you made of "good" or "bad" or "right" or "wrong" are not in alignment with your highest and best expression, the "pressures" will expel these covers and the misjudgment detaining You. You are aware, somewhere between this conscious level and the You that continues into the distance, that the premises you constructed behind "justice" and "fairness" call for reassessment so that the fuel for re-creation can flow and be assimilated within your Bodies. Your fervor in disorientation is your rallying to right a fundamental unfairness that does not exist. There is nothing unfair, intolerant, or condemning in deciding that explicit interests or opinions will inhibit your highest ambition, and not another's.

There are unimaginable variations of existence in equal or greater types of bodies, whether Light bodies or 3D bodies, along with furies of battling "truths" in the reaches of the All, tempests that restructure right from wrong with the best delivery of Love, and I must incorporate in my book of Rules what I am told is a fact while I can only see it as an opinion of another? With knowledge of this, does the I in the sky wish me to pack it up and carry it with me as "truth" that is incapable of changing!!!

The "truth" to your present condition will advance, adjust, and diversify for you as you morph again and again into updated versions of You.

When it is fundamental to you, the cause is never reexamined. Your well-rehearsed preoccupation does not situate well with Our chase for Your full presence on Terra, which remember, is unified within the conventions of the universes of the All. You will eventually join with the unimpaired balance of these edicts.

What society or fellow humans cumulatively decide to label "just" or "fair" or "humane" or "unjust", or "inhumane" is not a cause for all. On occasion, it is a hysteria which traps the unwary into following a framework that is not cut for their transitional progression. You called forth the Light brush of analysis by consenting to speculate on all your suppositions in Our "scorched Earth" survey of your ideological diagrams, which We know as affixed energies. You were not meant to ratify the postulations within the mass media's classroom or society's intonation of "correct," nor is any scholar of Earth. Each scholar's lessons, which are aimed at following an altered but upraised sense of their previous idea of reality, are as individual as each scholar's purpose. What persuades you with passionate announcements in the media are mostly not the universal certainties for which you have scouted Your Mountain. It is deluded ego, speculating on subjects in a narrow tunnel of thought. Society, current culture, and world leaders know not what scenery you drew upon just so that you might—with the eye of universal cannons burning in your ascension process—live a brighter day. Take note, when you portray the immense grandeur of the never-ending peaks with the valley attached, the comforting valley is what gives the mountains their majesty. Now, it is the mountain we are tending to.

Scripted scenes are meant for you, not another, to sort out the magnified You here on Terra. These same segments are the ideal mix for ruination if your inventiveness is not spacious enough to see the beneficial turn to be traversed in the landscapes of "just" and "fair." Right and wrong are easy to misunderstand when promoted with layers of severe emotions from times gone by. Pursue the metaphor: how does that stake you habitually drill into the ground to plant the idea of "justice" ring in the smooth wave of your "fair" heart as you pierce the soil? Is there rock, or soothing and moist soil? Does the Earth swallow the idea drilled into the area of the stake with certainty that the most nourishing supplements from far and wide will be obtainable to cultivate and nurture the planted idea?

The "justice" defined throughout the universe of untold reiterations of Light is the dominion to accredit the utmost respect. OUR role is to discover Our truths inherent within this Light and interpret all bearings on your journey through the use of the Light's prudence within your very Star. It is here that all of the aggregations of You will poke you for expanse. Short-sighted pronouncements from those with agendas to instill are not the system to counsel You in your estimate of the area in which to lay your stake. The severity of your clashes with the rocks, those bringing blisters to your hands, correlate directly to the miscalculation you amass around opinions as to the benefit or detriment of conduct or thought forms that may very well halt Our march toward reuniting Our whole.

You will not plunge your pilings into an Earth filled with gravel. WE both know the soil in which you dig. You have sown few crops that are resistant to Our conceptions. By the time the stalk has sprouted to the level at which it can thrive on your Light, this same Light having accumulated force, will have dispelled the occasional rock. The soil's makeup is a blend of your nobility in the universe, where you are the commander, issuing your regeneration.

PART XII: THE END

65: FROM CLEANSED VANTAGE POINTS

You who call yourself "Me" and "I," the "You" penetrating partially into Earth, I ask you to think it over; that is, think over what I bring to this partnership that my disincarnated version cannot spring into being with your most abject eagerness. I am here to act as an extract for Us. It is me who spawns the unmatched variants of this Love commodity and broadcasts them with a foresight so astonishing that they morph into an advanced substance applied by universal travelers to empower their entry into venues not available without my trials. Your disincarnated pokes and tugs for me to march on are stale without the tenets I sow while on Terra in cooperation with the Light of creation. Envisage this me appearing on the ground, how often I floated in the void of vulnerability, unclothed absent my faith that there is not a talent of broader magnitude than my ally with the Light's all-knowing and insulating sustenance. This I carried in the barren pit.

YOU, the I in the sky, tell your Terra twin here of the ultimate distant images You garnered from witnessing simultaneous existences while encased in an assailable and restrained vehicle of a body. Do I make my point? The one you call "Me," do you agree that this is outside of your scope? My extractions from the never-beginning or ending Light of love are entirely by way of cooperating as a ground force of the Light, like me. Bereft of me on the surface of the raging elements, your world is vacant and dim.

It is I who arouses You, my heavenly copy, when from a suspended absoluteness I form matter that lights Your world. It is referred to as traveling in the desertion of infinity. As I break the plane from security with the tangible into that which has no property of light, feeling, sound, or vibration, where I am hanging without weight or influence, I utter into the continuance a permanence, a resounding thought pulse borne from Earth, a triumph that my Transcended One cannot show for the All. YOU who profess to be the higher likeness of me in the superior realms do not have the prerogative to speculate on what it is to be perched in fractural flesh next to this doorway of nothingness and to stride into its center with the assurance of being established anew by way of immersing me into and out of this nullity of space while holding nothing other than Graces. What parallel experience does the I in the sky have to reference or correlate to so that You, my simile in the sky, may sense something like the air of obscurity, fear, confusion, and doubt which I thrive in the mist of? The immaculacy of a divine mode of being, one issuing from the interior of chaos, disturbance, and angst, can be correctly reported only from the script that I have the right to enact.

There it is! I jump into the result, an ancestor to the primal accent of love flaming with sights and smells of creation. These are the threads of infinity. That is the unrivaled dominance of being me here in the grimy zones of Terra.

I see the Now from reading between the Lines of Love. I am Love's experiment in the test tube of dirt, water, fire, and air.

The omnipotent aspect of loving kindness swells you with tremendous confidence when The Void is journeyed. WE both understand what true prosperity means, knowing that you have in "You" all there is need for in the abandonments of space. Rehearse these words in your mind to charge the signals beating in your Heart.

MY one wish I share with you in blessed simplicity is for you to trade places with Me for a flash of the timeless Now to live your Beingness from the other side of the shade of ignorance in stifling thoughts and there meet the Ruler for establishing all manners to reunite with your beautiful future, to meet Me, which is YOU.

Interspersed systems of linear filaments operating as precursors to potential events waver with each choice I make, while those holding a finer hue of indescribable elegance call all the others to their Bands of the native home, all constantly reflecting variant tones with each whirl that is connected to proceeding up Our mountain. As I evermore hold true to this optical wonder, I will question from my Heart the exact source of every implication embedded within my opinions formed in previous times, and will rob all words of the definitions borne from Earth's fears.

Are you sensing you are getting rolled into a false sense of security with Our communications? Well, if there is another one to the US, maybe you should reconsider your security. While there are many to help, it is solely the You of your Heart that you can have faith with. Your Star's highly tuned shine is that trust.

The End.

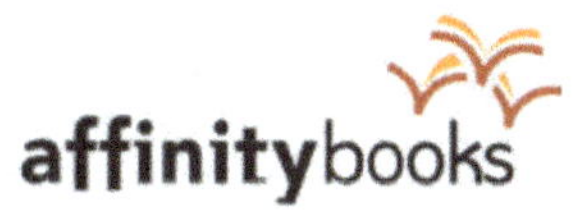

BIBLIOGRAPHY/CITATION TO AUTHORITY:

The only words taken from another author which are contained in this literature have been taken from:

1). The Buddha, Siddhārtha Gautama, Shakyamuni Buddha, who arrived on Earth on or about the period of 563 BCE. *The Buddha's words are paraphrased variously throughout this literature as: wishes for happiness and the causes of happiness for others/all sentient beings and for others/all sentient beings to be free from suffering and the causes of suffering.*

And 2).

The provoking Agent/Entity pushing revisions in resonance, "Max": "*Nothing Broken that Can't Be Fixed*" (page 176).

www.ingramcontent.com/pod-product-compliance
Lightning Source LLC
LaVergne TN
LVHW050515100826
845148LV00002B/339

* 9 7 8 0 6 9 2 9 8 4 3 3 8 *